# UPCYCLE

## A Modern Maker's Guide to Sewing and Mending a Preloved Wardrobe

Annie Phillips

**Photography by Kristen Perers**

quadrille

For our angel Sia x

# CONTENTS

# INTRODUCTION

Growing up, I was absolutely obsessed with crafts of all sorts, from painting to macramé. I wasn't particularly good at all of them, but between watching *Art Attack* on repeat, and with my grandma's help, I had soon fallen in love with anything DIY. My grandma has knitted and sewn for as long as I can remember, teaching and making my first handmade item with me and eventually giving me my first-ever shears. As a Ghanaian woman, having handmade clothes is integral to her cultural identity, with traditional cloths such as Kente, Adinkra and Batik fabrics holding significant cultural and historical value. This influence still plays a huge role in the designs I make to this day. Her mantra is and has always been '*nothing but the best*', and she still has some of these pieces in her wardrobe now, in her 90s, and she has a story to tell about every one of them. She would always tell me about what she was wearing at events, particularly in the Western world, and I could tell how important it was to her. It amuses me how she would catch people off-guard as their preconceptions didn't match the reality of the vibrant, intelligent young woman in front of them, completely at ease in surroundings not necessarily designed for her, because she was wearing '*nothing but the best*'. I think this is why I celebrate colour confidence and flamboyance so highly, because if you can't in this life when can you?

My other main influence has been my dad who, also like me, has always been a bit of a hoarder; coming home with boxes of people's unwanted possessions from his removal business, fixing projects (that never got fixed) and restoring classic cars back to life. Some of our most hilarious family anecdotes are those of when he has arrived home with 'something that might come in handy one day', with this once being a 2 m (6½ ft) Jesus statue that I still get a glimpse of if I look hard enough in the bushes of the garden. One of my first major 'projects' was completely redecorating the interior of my dad's 1970's VW campervan, me completely remaking the curtains and reupholstering the seats whilst my dad fixed the suspension and engine; neither of us really knowing what we were doing but winging it anyway. Surprisingly for us both, the results were so good that my gingham curtains are still on show to this day. Perhaps this is why it is second nature for me to see the beauty in the pre-loved. Whether it be vintage clothing, jewellery or second-hand furniture, I always find myself wondering where an item has come from, and the story it would tell if it could.

Forward to my 30s and after a long career in fashion buying, I quit to explore my newfound joy in sewing. Before starting this exciting journey, I had spent over a decade working for many high-street and designer brands, experiencing first-hand how fashion businesses drive their profits at the expense of the people who make the clothes, and our planet. Along the path of my career there was one stand-out moment for me. After building a relationship with one supplier in particular, I saw the impact fast fashion and the resultant worker exploitation had on families, who lost their homes, with many workers having to leave their children to live near the factory due to high order demands. The need for urgent and radical change was very clear to me. Maybe it was that I had just brought my own child into the world, or the uncertainty of the pandemic, maybe I was simply fatigued and disillusioned by the monotony of churning out trend after trend, but I knew that this was a broken system I could no longer be part of.

I delved further into the craft, meeting artisans all over the country, and after winning *The Great British Sewing Bee*, both my belief in myself, and my passion were reignited! I decided to look further into how we can make use of what we already have, and how, by educating others, I can help to reduce the demand for new products and the resources

required to manufacture them, by mending, altering and upcycling second-hand stuff. I also wanted to share this little happy place of mine: setting aside a project, putting on some music, and creating something beautiful – and how this could also lead the way for circularity and positive change. This book lets me share that happy place with you, and invites you to create one for yourself.

I believe that the ability to sew is crucial in creating a more sustainable industry; and a more sustainable approach to consumerism, one that prioritizes the planet and its resources, promoting a slower and more intentional approach to fashion, and – most importantly – encouraging us all to value high-quality, long-lasting garments over cheap, disposable ones, reducing the amount of textile waste that ends up in landfill. I am making it my mission to spread the sewing bug and put the power back in the consumer's hands by giving you the tools to increase the lifespan of your clothes. Plus, if you're anything like me, you'll be able to finally find a use for that shirt that's been sitting in your wardrobe since secondary school. Trust me, you'll thank yourself later when you're not standing there naked, holding onto the last shreds of your once-favourite top.

The fact that you have picked up this book tells me you have an interest in sewing already, and if not that, you are simply tired of the ill-fitting, bad-quality clothes out there right now. In this fast-paced society, never have we vaulted from one aesthetic to the next so quickly, and it can be hard for our wallets to keep up! Well don't worry honey, for I have the solution to all your fashion woes! With just a few basic hacks and a trusty sewing machine, you can create the wardrobe of your dreams (or nightmares, if you're into that kind of thing). This book will teach you how to create a more circular wardrobe with 'how-tos' on ways to repair and repurpose old clothes instead of purchasing new ones, and will enable you to create your own clothes, reducing your reliance on fast fashion. Plus, think of all the money you'll save on alterations and dry-cleaning bills! So come on, grab some fabric and a needle, and let's get sewing!

# How to use this book

This is your practical guide to DIYing your wardrobe to work for you, learning how to get that dopamine boost from reworking whatever treasures you may find in your drawers rather than in the high street!

Firstly, I start at the basics on your mission to mend, and then slowly guide you through the journey of refining your shopping habits, your approach to clothing and your wardrobe; clearing out the old, preparing you to rework your favourites into new, and learning how to care for the new wardrobe you love – ready to get crafty!

Then we can get practical! I have divided this book into three core chapters to upskill you from the sewing basics: upcycling the clothes you already own; creating something new from scratch; and mending. The majority of these tips and tricks are beginner-friendly to ignite the creativity inside you, but there are also some more challenging tasks to inspire those of you who already love sewing to try something new! I hope, if anything, that this book helps you take some time out from an incredibly busy life, to learn and try your hand at something mindful that can be a haven of calm and expressiveness in your everyday life.

My objective has always been to inspire the individuals who follow my journey to prioritize quality over quantity and to think about their consumption habits. This approach I hope will motivate people to value the pieces they buy or make and create lasting memories for years to come. As a conscious consumer, every purchase reflects your core values and I hope this book changes some attitudes so that more people can view shopping preloved – or indeed upcycling – as an opportunity to vote for the world you want to see. We are starting with a three-step plan for your wardrobe, helping you to reframe your approach to shopping, understand why you shop and why sometimes more isn't actually more. This will give you a baseline to identify what no longer serves you, which items can be got rid of and what is ready to be upcycled.

## Printing the patterns

Some of the projects in this book come with patterns, and you can access these using a QR code that can be found on the same page as the instructions.

The patterns are available to download and print as A4 or A0. It's important that you print the A4 patterns at 100% scale and select the setting for single-sided printing. Start by printing just one page with the test box on it. Measure the box to confirm that your settings are correct, and then, if you're happy that you don't need to adjust your printer settings, you can print the rest. Once printed, your pages will need to be carefully taped or glued together in the order shown in the guide, making sure that all the markings properly align.

Notice that the patterns are also available in A0 format. These can be printed by a professional printer on large sheets of paper, saving you the trouble of cutting and sticking, and saving on your home-printer inks too!

## Unravelling the art of sewing

Let's talk sewing. This isn't your average hobby, it's a tradition that goes way back, passed down through generations and filled with all sorts of fascinating history and creative brilliance. Here, we will delve into the origins of sewing and explore the basics – both for those of you only just embarking on this exciting journey, and for those who have already begun!

Sewing has been a part of human life for thousands of years. We're talking back to the early Stone Age, when our ancestors made needles made from bones or animal horns and then used them to sew leather or furs together. These early techniques gradually evolved, resulting in more refined stitching methods throughout the ages to the shiny metal needles we use now!

But it wasn't just our Stone Age friends getting crafty. In Egypt, garments were essential for personal protection and ceremonial purposes. Intricate stitching techniques were employed to create elaborate garments, including the iconic pleated and embroidered robes seen in Ancient Egyptian art. Similarly, the Greeks were known for their unique draping and sewing methods, with fabrics often flowing gracefully to evoke a sense of beauty and elegance. I think this shows just how much the outcome can change depending on the artist behind the needle.

Sewing is a remarkable art form rooted in ancient traditions, ever evolving to cater to contemporary creativity. With a rich history and endless possibilities, I believe it offers a wonderful outlet for self-expression and personal style. So, gather your tools, select your perfect fabric, and let your imagination soar as you embark on your sewing journey. Just remember, with this book, you can make each project your own depending on the fabrics and style that suits you.

# MASTERING THE BASICS

Embarking on the journey of sewing can seem intimidating, but don't worry! Here are some basic steps to get you started. It is essential if you have not sewn before to familiarize yourself with these steps and practise the basic stitches. These will allow you to create secure seams, apply decorative elements, and gain an understanding of what's to come! If you're impatient like me, don't worry – this should only take a short amount of time to get your head around.

Experiment with various techniques to enhance your skills. If you really love your first few projects and want to upskill, get a friend to help you, or even join a class or local sewing group, which can provide invaluable guidance and inspiration and also some good sewing company!

## Hand sewing

Hand sewing is the foundation of sewing and enables you to create precise, delicate and artistic details. First thread a needle and make a knot at the end of the thread.

**Tacking (basting) stitch:**
This is the most basic stitch commonly used to hold pieces of fabric together temporarily but more securely than pinning. It is a simple up-and-down stitch that creates a straight line. Firstly, thread a needle in a contrast thread so you will be able to see the stitches easily and make a knot at the end. Pass the needle through the fabric from the bottom and then bring it back up again. Repeat this motion, making fairly large stitches, until the desired length of seam is achieved. These stitches are usually removed when the final seam is sewn.

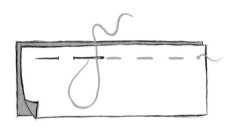

**Running stitch:**
A quick and easy stitch used for decoration or joining seams. Begin by bringing the needle up through the fabric and then insert it back down a small distance away – it's just like tacking (basting) but the stitches are smaller. Repeat this motion, creating evenly spaced stitches.

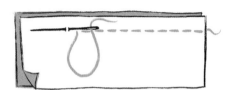

### Whipstitch:

Whipstitching is a simple and effective hand-sewing technique that can be used for sewing on trims or appliqués or for joining the edges of a turning gap, for example when making a bag like the lined tote. To whipstitch, first align the edges of the two fabrics you want to stitch together. Insert your needle from the wrong side of the fabric, coming out near the edge of the fabric. Take a small stitch over the edge through both layers of fabric, keeping the stitches close together. Repeat this process, just catching the edge of the fabric with each stitch, until you reach the end. Finally, knot the thread securely and trim any excess.

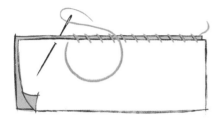

### Backstitch:

Bring the needle through the fabric from the back to the front at the starting point of your stitching. Pull the thread until the knot stops at the back. Next, insert the needle back into the fabric a stitch length behind the starting point, and pull the thread until it is taut. Bring the needle up again a stitch length in front of the first stitch. Now, insert the needle back into the fabric at the end point of the previous stitch and bring it out again a stitch length ahead of the second stitch. Repeat these steps, making sure the stitches are of even length and form a continuous line, and the fabric remains taut. The resulting backstitch will have a solid, strong line of stitches perfect for securing fabric edges.

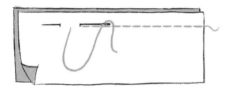

### Hemming stitch:

Ideal for hemming garments or fabric edges. Fold the fabric edge twice to create a clean hem. Starting from inside the folded edge, bring the needle up, catch only a few threads on the front layer, and then insert it back into the fold. Repeat this uniformly, making small stitches that show as little as possible on the right side.

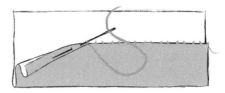

## Machine stitches and techniques

### (J & K) Straight stitch:

The most common stitch used in sewing projects. Set your sewing machine to a straight stitch setting. Place the fabric under the needle and lower the presser foot. Start sewing slowly and guide the fabric straight through the machine, keeping a consistent seam allowance (the width from the fabric edge).

### (H & I) Zigzag stitch:

Used for finishing edges, preventing fraying, and sewing stretch fabrics. Set your machine to the zigzag stitch setting. Place the fabric under the needle and lower the presser foot. Start sewing; you feed the fabric through as normal, and the machine does the 'side-to-side' to create a zigzag pattern.

### (G) Tacking (basting) stitch:

Temporary stitches used for fitting or holding fabric layers together. Set your machine to a longer stitch length. Place the fabric under the needle and lower the presser foot. Sew straight, but avoid backstitching at the beginning and end so you can easily remove the stitches later.

A   B   C   D   E   F   G H   I   J   K

**Buttonhole stitch:**
Used for creating buttonholes. Set your sewing machine to the buttonhole stitch setting. Attach the buttonhole presser foot and lower the foot. For some machines you can put the button in the buttonhole foot so that it can automatically measure how long the hole needs to be. If not, you will need to measure this. Follow the machine instructions to sew the buttonhole, usually by selecting the desired buttonhole length and width on your machine.

**(F) Blind hem stitch:**
Ideal for invisible hemming on garments. Set your machine to the blind hem stitch setting. Fold the fabric edge to create a small hem, and then fold the hem under the main fabric so just the edge shows. Place the fabric under the presser foot with the straight edge against the guide. Start sewing slowly, ensuring the machine stitches catch the folded edge only on the wide stitches, to leave small, almost invisible stitches on the garment's right side.

**(D & E) Overlock stitch:**
Used for finishing raw edges and sewing seams in one step. Set your machine to the overlock stitch setting or use an overlock (serger) machine. Place the fabric under the needle and lower the presser foot. Sew along the fabric edge, allowing the machine to create stitches that encase the edge to prevent fraying. This gives a professional finish, but if you do not have this option on your machine, or an overlocker, you can use a zigzag stitch the same way.

**(C) Stretch stitch:**
Designed for sewing stretch fabrics like knits. Set your machine to the stretch stitch setting. Place the fabric under the needle and lower the presser foot. Start sewing slowly, following the machine's stretch stitch pattern, usually a combination of straight and zigzag stitches to allow the fabric to stretch without breaking the stitches. Do not pull the fabric through the machine but allow the feed dogs to move it without stretching.

**(A & B) Satin stitch**
Ideal for decorative edges and appliqué work. Set your machine to the satin stitch setting or a dense zigzag stitch. Place the fabric under the needle and lower the presser foot. Sew slowly, guiding the fabric as the needle moves from side to side to create a solid stitch line.

**Topstitching:**
Topstitching is a decorative and functional technique where stitches are placed on the outside of a garment, often parallel or close to the seam. It adds strength, stability and a professional look to the finished piece (think of the orange stitching on your jeans). To achieve topstitching, sew along the desired edge or fold, keeping the stitching straight and parallel. Control the stitch distance from the edge by aligning the fabric with a guide on the machine. You may want to use a slightly thicker topstitching thread to do this and a longer stitch to help the stitches stand out.

**Decorative stitches:**
Your machine may come with a variety of built-in decorative stitches that can be fun to incorporate into your creations. The best way to learn about these - and all the other stitches your machine can sew - is to get a piece of fabric and try them out (see page 15). Even some of the practical stitches can be used decoratively if you use a little imagination.

# Sewing techniques

 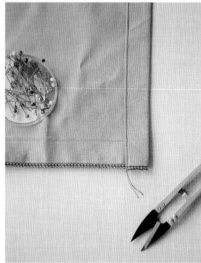

**Hemming:**
Hemming is the process of folding over the raw edge of a fabric and stitching it in place to create a neat and finished edge. It is important because it prevents fraying and gives a polished look to garments. To achieve a basic double hem, fold the edge of the fabric towards the wrong side twice and sew it down with a straight stitch. Alternatively, use your blind hem stitch for a less visible hem, or even sew it by hand.

**Gathering:**
Gathering involves stitching two parallel rows of stitches within the seam allowance to create even and controlled folds or gathers. This technique is essential for creating ruffles, gathers on sleeves, or adding fullness to skirts or dresses. To gather the fabric, gently pull the bobbin threads to evenly distribute the gathers.

**Sewing darts:**

Darts are folds in fabric that provide shape to a garment, particularly around curves like the bust, waist, or hips. They help create a more tailored and fitted look by removing excess fabric. To sew a dart, mark the placement on the fabric, fold it along the centre of the dart, and stitch from the wide end to the narrow end, creating a triangle of fabric on the wrong side of the garment.

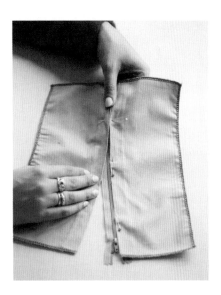

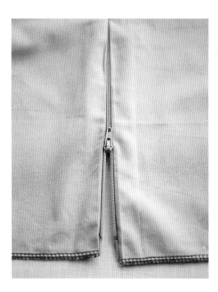

**Adding a zip:**

Zips (zippers) are essential for closures in garments, bags, or other sewn items. To add a zip, start by marking the placement on the fabric and sewing the seam until the point where the zip will be inserted. Then, pin the zip face-down on the seam from the wrong side and sew it in place with a straight stitch using a zip foot, going slowly and carefully to ensure even stitching on both sides. If your zip is longer than required, you can easily just cut off the excess once it's sewn in place.

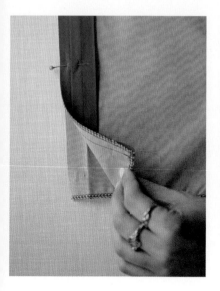

**Adding bias binding:**
Open out one edge of the bias binding and place it on the edge to be bound. Fold over the starting end to hide the raw edge. Sew in place with a straight stitch along the fold line on the binding, and when you get round to the beginning again, overlap the folded end and trim off any excess binding. Then fold the binding over raw fabric edge(s) to enclose them and sew in place on the other side. If you don't want any stitching to show on the right side, it is better to hand sew the second side using hemming stitch (see page 14). After you finish sewing, trim off the excess threads. The image showcases binding used to cover seams, but you can follow this same technique on one layer of fabric to cover the neckline.

# Things You Need

To begin sewing, you'll need some essential tools and some useful extras, including:

**Sewing machine:**
It's important here that you choose wisely! I'd try a second-hand machine if you are just starting out, but the maintenance of a machine is vital so I would recommend investing in one of your own if you fall in love with the craft. It doesn't have to be expensive, just cleaned regularly to get rid of any stray threads or fluff, particularly in the bobbin case. Make sure you ensure your machine can do all of the stitches you need as some only will do a straight stitch. Key functions to look out for would be zigzag stitch, buttonholes and stretch stitch.

**Needles:**
Hand-sewing and machine needles, the sharper the better! With machine needles, purple-tip needles are fantastic for most fabrics, whether that be stretch, cotton or something a little heavier. But do remember you may need to go for a heavy-duty needle if you are sewing with something very thick, or microtext needles if you are sewing with something very thin or delicate like satin.

**Fabrics:**
Try to use second-hand or offcuts where possible that you have gathered from your unwanted wardrobe. Initially use stable cotton because it is much easier to sew and will not slip under the machine. I personally love using African wax prints/batik fabrics for this reason as they are sturdy, often cotton and easy to press. I also love working with textured fabrics like fluffy faux furs, sparkly or embroidered fabrics – but be aware that the more textured the fabrics, the harder they are to sew as they are often bumpier and bulkier. The more experienced you get, the more you will be able to handle something a little more complex!

**Threads:**
The closer the colour is to the colour of your fabric, the more invisible the stitching will be. To start with, go for a white and black to match back to light or dark fabrics, and if you are planning to continue I'd recommend investing in a range of colours to match back to the colours of your fabrics.

**Scissors and snips:**
You will need separate fabric and paper scissors as you want the fabric scissors to remain nice and sharp for easy cutting, plus snips or small scissors for trimming  threads. If you are more advanced, why not even try a rotary cutter!

**Seam ripper:**
This is to unpick mistakes or the original stitching of a garment – so is a must-have for upcycling.

**Iron and ironing board:**
To make sure the fabric is crease-free and those seams are neat and pressed.

**Air- or water-soluble marker or chalk:**
You will need to mark some of the positions on the pattern onto the fabric to make it much easier whilst cutting or sewing.

**Pins or clips:**
To hold the seams together before you stitch them. I prefer to go old-school with pins and a pincushion.

**Measuring tape and dressmaker's ruler:**
A measuring tape is an essential to any sewing kit, and if you take your sewing further, a dressmaker's pattern ruler will help you draft your own designs.

**Safety pins and loop turner:**
Use safety pins to feed things like elastic through channels, while a loop turner will help you turn narrow straps and ties right side out.

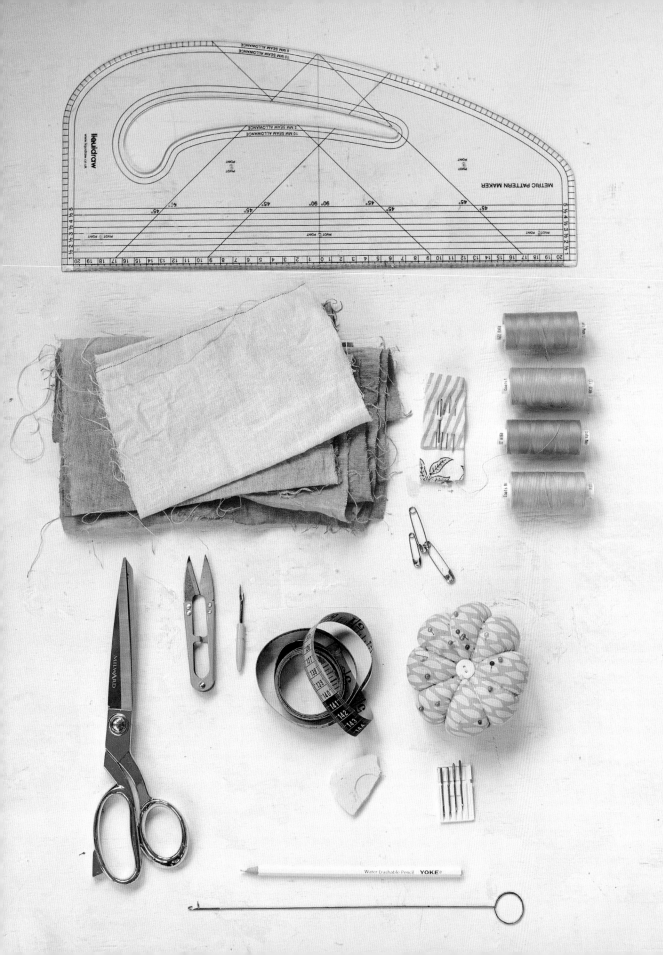

# THE POWER OF REPAIRING AND UPCYCLING

So why bother with repairs? Well, first and foremost I believe it's a wonderful way for us to express our creativity and individuality. Repairing clothing allows for amazing customization, enabling us to adjust the fit, add embellishments, or repurpose items entirely. Just think, these are the techniques that brought us some of the most exciting fashion over time (hello punk era). By transforming old garments, we can cultivate our unique sense of style and stand out from the crowd, whilst encouraging a greater appreciation for the art of making and mending, fostering a deeper connection to our clothing and accessories.

Now, let's talk about the economic benefits. Repairing and upcycling your clothes can be a super smart and budget-friendly move. On average, households in the UK spend about 4% of their budget on clothing and footwear. That's roughly £25 a week, £109 a month, and a whopping £1,308 a year. In the USA the average spend is $1500 annually. So by repairing your clothes instead of buying new ones, you could save a ton of money. Not only that, but the repair and upcycling industry can also create job opportunities and give local economies a boost. So it's not just good for your wallet, but for your community, too.

Now, on to the heavy stuff. As we all know, the fashion industry is a major contributor to global pollution and waste, which is pretty alarming. Check out these stats:

+ Can you believe that a huge 85% of textile waste each year ends up in landfills or gets burned, which releases greenhouse gases? That's a lot!

+ According to the Ellen MacArthur Foundation, the fashion industry is responsible for about 10% of global carbon emissions. Yep, that's even more than international flights and shipping combined.

+ And don't forget about all the water, energy, and chemicals needed to produce new textiles. By 2022, it's reported that 113.8 million metric tonnes (125.4 million US tons) of new textile fibres were produced. Natural fibres such as cotton or wool had a production volume of 25.2 million metric tonnes (27.78 million US tons), while synthetic fibres accounted for the remaining 87.6 million (96.6 million US), which is not great for the environment at all. But by repairing and upcycling clothes, we can break this wasteful cycle. We can extend the life of our garments, reduce the need for new ones, and even cut down on landfill waste. It's a win-win!

We all know of the horrors of fast fashion, but sustainable fashion has been gaining serious traction lately as we all start to think more about the environmental impact of our clothing choices. You know those labels that claim their clothes are made from recycled bottles? Have you ever wondered what that really means, or if it's actually better for the environment? For example, did you know that officially, 'a yarn can only be branded "recycled" when spun with more than 20% recycled fibres?' But even with recycled plastics used in clothing, the fibres continue shedding from recycled plastic yarns just as much as from virgin yarns, polluting waterways.

These brands know the psychology behind why people buy and the power of marketing, and when you delve into the facts it's pretty fascinating. There is a natural tendency for individuals to seek pleasure and avoid pain, and shopping often provides a sense of gratification. When people

buy something, dopamine – a neurotransmitter associated with pleasure and reward – is released in the brain, creating a pleasurable sensation. This biologically-driven response plays a significant role in the consumer behaviour of seeking that feel-good experience. The power of marketing amplifies this effect by strategically enticing consumers to make purchases.

Marketers create a sense of urgency, exclusivity, and status around products, manipulating the consumer's needs. This is made even clearer in the constant introduction of fashion seasons. By creating new collections and fostering real FOMO, we're driven to keep up with the latest trends and engage in repeated shopping habits. The intertwining of psychology and marketing promotes a never-ending cycle of consumption, fuelled by the desire for that dopamine kick and the fear of falling behind. However, as consumers, we're becoming more aware of the importance of sustainability. And many fashion brands are catching on to this trend and trying to make their products seem eco-friendly. But not all of them are actually promoting genuine sustainable practices as we saw in our examples earlier. It's called greenwashing, and it's pretty sneaky.

The problem is that terms like 'sustainable' and 'eco-friendly' don't have legal definitions. This means brands can make vague claims without any proof. According to the UK Consumer Protection Partnership, about 40% of environmental claims in advertisements are misleading or downright false. Talk about confusing! Luckily, more regulations are being gradually put in place, but transparency is key to truly sustainable fashion. Unfortunately, many greenwashing brands don't provide enough information about their supply chains,

manufacturing processes, or where they source their materials. According to a survey by Fashion Revolution, only 35% of UK-based fashion brands disclose their supplier lists. So we actually have no idea where, or how, the clothes they produce are made. Certification programs such as the Global Organic Textile Standard (GOTS) or the Textile Exchange certify products as sustainable. Unfortunately, a mere 2% of global textile fibre production adheres to these standards, suggesting that many claims of sustainability by fashion brands are generally unfounded.

To truly be sustainable, the fashion industry needs to embrace the circular economy. It's all about minimizing waste and making the most of our resources. But unfortunately, many brands don't follow this principle. Greenpeace found that only 1% of fashion items globally are recycled into new clothing. That's a whole lot of wasted potential! The fashion industry has the power to make a real change when it comes to sustainability, but until they keep up we must take the first step ourselves. Repairing and upcycling clothes are simple yet effective strategies to reduce waste, cut carbon emissions, and create a more environmentally friendly and economically viable future. Let's embrace our creativity, reimagine our wardrobes and be a part of the sustainable fashion revolution. It's time to make some real positive change!

# 1

# Love your clothes *for longer*

So how does looking after your clothes make them last longer? We've all been there: when we purchase new clothes, we often envision ourselves wearing them for a long time, cherishing each piece and getting the most out of our investment. However, many of us unknowingly neglect the simple practices that can significantly prolong the lifespan of our garments and our favourite jumper ends up bobbled and scrunched up in the bottom of our wardrobe (yes, I'm looking at you!). By adopting a few good habits and taking some extra care, we can ensure that our clothes remain in excellent condition and last longer.

Before living with my partner, I thought everyone knew the basics of laundry (until I ended up with all of my whites a faint blue colour), so please excuse me if this sounds a little elementary but we're going to start at the basics. Sorting them correctly before washing is crucial. Separate light and dark colours because dyed fabrics may release colour during laundering. If you only have a small amount of one group, don't be tempted to put it in with another – save it for a full load. If you have a fabric with a white background and pattern, this can be a bit more tricky! I personally would then go the extra mile, and not mix it with the dazzling whites

## Natural stain removers

**Tea or coffee stains:** Act quickly by pouring boiling water over the stain until it disappears. If the stain is already set, scrub it with a mixture of borax and water, then wash the garment right away.

**Grass stains:** Scrub with liquid dish soap or treat the area with a 50/50 mix of 3% hydrogen peroxide and water.

**Mud stains:** Let the stain dry and brush off what you can. Then, scrub it with a borax/water paste and wash it immediately.

**Tomato-based stains:** Treat the area with white vinegar and wash it immediately.

**Dingy whites or underarm deodorant stains:** Mix a solution of equal parts: one part 3% hydrogen peroxide, one part baking soda and one part water. I'd suggest 30ml (⅛ cup) of each for one t-shirt. Apply directly to the stain and let it soak for 30 minutes. For stubborn yellow stains, create a paste with 3% hydrogen peroxide and baking soda, gently scrub it onto the stain, and let it sit for 5 minutes before washing.

**Other food stains:** Treat with a 50/50 mix of 3% hydrogen peroxide and water and soak.

**Grease and oil stains:** Sprinkle the stain with dry bicarbonate of soda to remove any loose oil or grease and brush it off. Then, soak in undiluted white vinegar for 15 minutes and rinse and scrub with liquid dish soap before washing.

**Bodily fluids (vomit, urine, blood) or protein-based stains (egg, gelatine, glue):** Soak in cool water (not warm/hot water as this traps in the odour). Then wash in the washing machine with an additional mixture of half a cup of hydrogen peroxide and half a cup of bicarbonate of soda.

because the colours may still run, so I would create a light wash with light colours. Additionally, sorting by fabric type, such as delicate or heavy fabrics, prevents damage from occurring. This practice ensures a gentle wash for delicate fabrics and helps prevent snagging, pilling, or stretching.

Frequent washing can also take a toll on clothing, so whenever possible, avoid laundering unnecessarily. Hanging clothes outside in fresh air can freshen them up and reduce the need for washing. When removing your clothes, make sure to hang or fold them neatly to avoid wrinkles or stretching (i.e. not in a pile in the corner of the bedroom). It's also great to get into the habit of using a clothing brush, especially for jackets or velvet. This removes dust and debris from clothes without needing to wash them, which saves water and energy.

Where possible, washing clothes in cold water helps clothes retain their colour and prevents shrinking. It also saves energy, because hot water uses more energy to heat up. I always think to myself, would I wash my face or body in 90-degree water? No? So, is it really necessary for clothes that you've worn once or twice? Equally, avoid using a dryer and opt for hanging clothes to dry or lay them flat. This saves energy and prevents shrinkage or damage from high heat.

The most critical factor in maintaining the quality of your clothes is proper laundering. Always read the care instruction labels sewn inside your garments and follow them. Different fabrics and colours require different care methods, so pay close attention. Using the appropriate washing machine setting and temperature, and choosing the right detergent can eliminate the risk of permanent damage. Using a gentle laundry detergent is preferred because harsh detergents can damage fibres and shorten the life of your clothes. Look for eco-friendly brands or those without chemicals such as phosphates.

Dealing with stains promptly is another way to extend the lifespan of your clothes. Treating stains as soon as possible reduces the chances of them becoming permanent. Always read the care instructions before applying any stain-removal techniques, ensuring compatibility with the fabric. There are numerous natural and store-bought stain removers available so finding a suitable option for each type of stain should be relatively easy, or alternatively you can use natural stain removers like lemon juice or bicarbonate of soda (baking soda). You can always refer to my guide of natural stain removers if you are in doubt!

Taking the time to properly store your clothes is equally essential. Prioritize hanging clothes to help maintain their shape. Investing in quality hangers that suit various types of garments will provide additional support and reduce the risk of stretching or misshaping, particularly for heavy items like coats or jackets. For delicate fabrics prone to wrinkles, folding and storing them flat in drawers or on shelves can be helpful.

Lastly, regular maintenance and garment inspections are essential – there's more about this in the section starting on page 128. Mend small tears or loose buttons immediately to prevent further damage. Check your clothes from time to time for signs of wear or damage, such as thinning fabric, loose threads, or any areas that need reinforcement. Timely repairs can help prevent minor issues from becoming irreparable, extending the life of your clothes. For thicker fabrics, use a fabric shaver to remove pills and fuzz that can make clothes look worn and old.

By adopting these habits, you can ensure that the clothes you love will continue to serve you well for years to come.

## Summary:

+ Wash clothes less frequently

+ Wash on a cold wash

+ Act quickly on stains by spot cleaning

+ Store clothes properly with correct hangers

+ Use a gentle laundry detergent

+ Avoid using a dryer – hang clothes or lay them to dry flat

**Extra Susty Tips:**

+ Use eco-friendly laundry detergents

+ Use wool dryer balls instead of dryer sheets

+ Use a washing bag to prevent microfibres from entering waterways

+ Avoid using bleach

+ Use natural stain removers (see the list opposite)

# 2 Refine
## your wardrobe

This step is crucial, and I hate to be the bearer of bad news, but this won't be quick, so set aside an afternoon or evening for this task! However, it will ultimately save you a significant amount of time on a daily basis, because you'll easily be able to find the clothes that work for you, feel fabulous in them, and rediscover your excitement for your wardrobe. If you follow me on social media – and hey, if you do, you'll know that I am far from minimalist – you'll already be aware that I see refining my wardrobe as an ongoing process. Now I know it can be overwhelming being surrounded by your entire wardrobe at once, but this time we have a process!

The ultimate aim is to have a well-organized wardrobe that is easy to navigate. Once everything is in front of you, make the effort to try on each item. While this may be time-consuming, it's essential for effectively sorting the items into four separate groups. If you tend to struggle with indecisiveness, consider bringing a trusted bestie along to provide advice and support. A 'sip and sort' evening, even! By going through this process, we not only achieve a fabulous wardrobe but also identify items that can be repurposed or repaired, adding new excitement to our collection. Let's get started:

**My wardrobe staples:**
These are the pieces you wear repeatedly, regardless of the season. They should match your lifestyle and aesthetic, and be of good quality. As an additional tip, when shopping, prioritize investing in this category. If there are items you constantly wear but are of poor quality or made from synthetic materials, consider replacing them with higher-quality pieces. These wardrobe staples should make up 70% of your overall collection.

**Things that bring me joy:**
These are the standout pieces, such as a gorgeous dinner dress or abstract jumper that you fell in love with. However, they must fit you properly, be wearable, and have been worn within the last 6 months. These items should account for around 30% of your wardrobe, as they are worn less frequently. Nonetheless, having these unique pieces is essential for adding excitement and variety to your wardrobe.

**Items that require altering, mending, or repairing:**
This category includes items like too-long trousers or beloved pieces that need some TLC. Is there a non-functioning zip, a hole in your favourite jumper, a stressed seam, or a stain on your go-to top? We are going to make these pieces wearable again. Often, we set them aside, intending to eventually repair them, but it never happens. Take this opportunity to tackle all these adjustments at once. Reinvesting in your own wardrobe is not only a responsible way to handle your purchases, but it's also cost-effective and promotes sustainability. This category focuses on returning items to their original condition, making them feel brand new.

**Things that no longer serve me:**
These are the jeans that no longer fit, the dress that doesn't flatter your current shape or taste, or the items that haven't been worn in years. In my case, after having my son, I found that many of the dresses I used to wear no longer worked for my changed body shape or new lifestyle. As a result, even after a year, many of my favourite repeat dresses were still untouched in my wardrobe. It was time for them to go. With this pile, you'll need to set aside anything you wish to donate, give to charity, or send for recycling. Please note that if an item has a hole or stain, it cannot be resold by a charity shop, and it will likely end up dumped in places like Kantamanto Market in Accra (which is not what we want!). In fact, according to a 2019 report from the Environmental Audit Committee, only about 30% of donations are actually resold within the UK. Therefore, this step requires some careful consideration.

Firstly, identify and set aside anything that excites you in some way. Is it an interesting print, a beautiful fabric colour, or a unique jeans wash? These items can be upcycled and repurposed.

Next, evaluate the remaining items to determine what is still wearable and suitable for selling on a second-hand platform, donating to charity or friends, what can be recycled (these must be single-fibre only fabrics), and what is truly waste.

Now I know this step is easier said than done sometimes. Letting go of a wardrobe can be an unexpectedly emotional task. It entails more than simply parting with clothes that no longer fit or suit our style, but it can be a mentally heavy process to hoard clothing items that once held sentimental value or represented a different version of ourselves. As we come to terms with the physical changes in our bodies or the evolution of our personal style, we realize that holding onto these garments only hinders our growth. Letting go allows someone else to find joy in these clothes and enables us to embrace our present selves, ultimately lightening the weight on our shoulders and making space for new possibilities. I always repeatedly say to myself... they're just clothes! The memories will always remain. So, now that we have a better understanding of what we already own, let's learn how to adopt a more mindful approach to future purchases.

# 3

# Learn how to shop

*more sustainably*

Day in and day out I speak to people about 'sustainability' and in today's rapidly evolving world, it has become an increasingly crucial aspect of our daily lives. As consumers, we hold immense power to shape the future by making conscious choices when shopping. Now that we've learnt how to care for the clothes we love, and to refine our wardrobe, we need to know how to maintain this and shop more consciously. By adopting sustainable shopping practices, we can reduce our carbon footprint and support the businesses that prioritize ethical practices and social responsibility, just like us! I'm going to give you my top five valuable tips to

help you shop with all of this in mind, and make a positive impact on the planet. I've also added a little go-to guide if you're at the checkout thinking about it and panicking, to help you decide whether to go ahead with the purchase!

**Embrace the thrift revolution:**
One of the most effective ways to shop sustainably is by not buying new at all. By exploring the world of thrift and second-hand, you contribute to reducing waste and the demand for new production. Thrift shopping allows you to discover unique pieces while supporting local charities or contributing to circular

economies. Check out the guide for making sure you are buying quality second-hand items on page 37 before you go ahead, and have fun with it!

## Reduce, reuse, recycle:

Following the three Rs is a simple yet powerful mantra for sustainable shopping. Before making a purchase, ask yourself if you truly need the item or if it can be borrowed, rented, or shared with others. If you already own something similar, consider repurposing or upcycling it instead of buying something new. When disposing of items, recycle whenever possible, and always consider donating or selling unwanted items before sending them to landfill.

## Support ethical brands:

Do your research. Look for brands that prioritize ethical practices and sustainability. Many companies have incorporated environmentally friendly processes, fair-trade policies, and ethical sourcing into their production chain but to be sure, look for certifications such as Fair Trade, GOTS (Global Organic Textile Standard), or B-Corp. These assure that a brand is committed to sustainable practices. By supporting ethical brands, you vote with your wallet for a better future. And if you are really unsure, I would check if the brand is listed on the Fashion Transparency Index, which highlights the gap between brand claims and actions towards circularity.

## Invest in quality and longevity:

In a world of fast fashion and disposable goods, it's important to prioritize quality over quantity. Check the care label for the materials used. Opt for well-made, durable fabrics that will stand the test of time. Once you have started your sewing journey you will find it easier to spot the rubbish; the bad, inconsistent stitching, the mismatched seams or the fraying that will only get worse after one wash. Investing in quality items reduces the need for frequent replacements and consequently reduces waste.

## Go with a plan:

Think about how this item fits into your newly refined wardrobe. I tend to go shopping with what I need in mind because it helps me stay focused and find exactly what I need. Doing the same will allow you to prioritize your shopping list and avoid impulsive purchases. Think about how often you will wear this piece and many other items it goes with. By choosing something that is timeless to you, you can avoid falling into temporary fashion trends, thus minimizing the impact of your wardrobe on the environment. Additionally, having a plan can save you time and prevent you from getting overwhelmed by what feels like a gigantic wardrobe in some second-hand stores.

Shopping sustainably is not just a passing trend; it's a conscious choice that empowers us to make a positive impact on the environment. By embracing the tips mentioned above, you can reduce your carbon footprint, support ethical brands, and minimize waste. Remember, every small step matters, and collectively, we can create a more sustainable future. Let's make a difference through conscious consumerism.

## To buy or not to buy

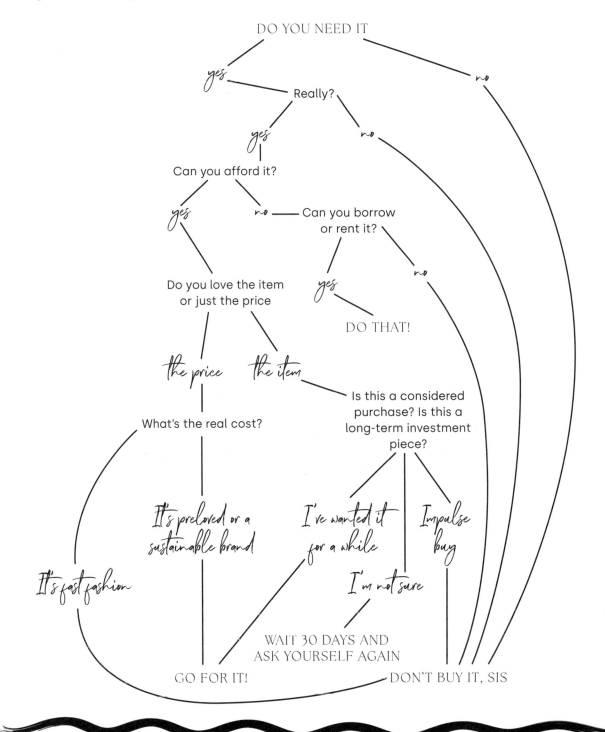

DO YOU NEED IT

*yes* — Really?

*no*

Really?

*yes* — Can you afford it?

*no*

Can you afford it?

*yes* — Do you love the item or just the price

*no* — Can you borrow or rent it?

Can you borrow or rent it?

*yes* — DO THAT!

*no*

Do you love the item or just the price

*the price* — What's the real cost?

*the item* — Is this a considered purchase? Is this a long-term investment piece?

What's the real cost?

*It's fast fashion*

*It's preloved or a sustainable brand*

Is this a considered purchase? Is this a long-term investment piece?

*I've wanted it for a while*

*I'm not sure*

*Impulse buy*

WAIT 30 DAYS AND ASK YOURSELF AGAIN

GO FOR IT!

DON'T BUY IT, SIS

# Signs of Good Quality Pre-Loved Items

**The fabric:**
Look for fabrics that feel soft to the touch, hold their shape well and don't look worn or faded. Check the composition. Natural fibres are biodegradable and ecologically sustainable, while plastics like polyester take hundreds of years to decompose, polluting the environment. Natural fibres have better breathability than synthetic fibres, allowing air to circulate more freely, which helps in moisture absorption and reduces odours. They also offer superior comfort, as they feel more pleasant on the skin than synthetic fibres, which can cause irritation and sweating. Natural fibres have higher absorbency than synthetic fibres, so they can absorb more moisture before feeling damp, which makes them a popular choice for clothing, and they are less likely to cause skin allergies or respiratory problems, because they don't contain harmful chemicals or artificial dyes, unlike synthetic fibres. Also, choose high-quality fabrics, trims, and accessories to ensure their longevity and durability.

**Care instructions:**
Look at the care instructions on the label. If it requires dry cleaning or hand washing, it's likely to be of higher quality than items that can be machine washed.

**Attention to detail:**
Every aspect of a garment's construction process must be scrutinized, from the choice of thread to the placement of zips and buttons. Every stitch should be precise, and no loose threads should be left dangling. Make sure collars lay flat and aren't too stretched out or wrinkled. Look for garments with a lining – it adds durability and makes clothing feel more luxurious. Make sure buttons are secure and in good condition. Check zips to ensure they slide easily and are in good condition. The hardware should be smooth when used i.e. no sticking zip teeth!

**Skilled craftsmanship:**
Garment construction is a dead giveaway; it requires skilled hands with years of experience in stitching, cutting, and finishing techniques to make quality garments. Every seam should meet precisely, hems should be straight, and seam edges should be cleanly finished. Check the seams to make sure they are straight, properly stitched, and not pulling or puckering. Look at the bottom hem to see if it's even and clean. Uneven or frayed hemlines can be a sign of a low-quality garment.

**Brand:**
Check for quality brands that are known for their high-quality materials and construction. Consider the reputation of the brand. A brand with a long history of producing high-quality products tends to command higher prices, and items made with high-quality materials and meticulous attention to detail will likely demonstrate their quality through their durability and craftsmanship. Fast-fashion brands are not designed to stand the test of time, whereas garments that are considered vintage and remain in good condition are likely to be of superior quality and continue to last well.

**Consistent sizing and fitting:**
Garment construction should ensure that each piece is consistently sized and that it fits correctly. Manufacturers should adhere to strict quality-control procedures to maintain a consistent sizing and fitting experience.

Upcy

cling

Adding
a waist
p48

Adding a
trim p44

Sweater
to vest *p52*

Balaclava
*p56*

# Patchwork
# Dad shirt

*p60*

# Tablecloth
# to dress *p64*

# Three T-shirt
upcycles p74

# Jeans
## to skirt
p70

# Adding
## a trim

The easiest update, adding a quick trim can really be a game changer when turning something from old to new. Think party, feathers or a contrast of colour to pop on your existing trousers, shirt cuffs or dresses to level up your everyday wardrobe. You can even give this a go with your accessories!

## Things You'll Need

**Item to trim**
**Measuring tape**
**Trim (in this example I've used feathers)**
**Scissors**
**Pins or clips**
**Hand sewing needle**
**Thread in coordinating colour**

## Technique

**Prepare the item and the trim:**

1   Lay the garment flat on a table or a flat surface with the edge you wish to attach the trim to facing up.

2   Measure and cut a piece of trim slightly longer than the length of the garment edge, allowing for some extra room to work with. It's always better to have a little extra trim than to come up short.

3   Position the trim along the edge of the garment, aligning it evenly. Pin the trim in place at intervals, securing it temporarily to prevent it from shifting during sewing.

**Begin sewing:**

**4**  Thread the needle with a suitable length of thread that matches the trim and double it up to make it stronger. Secure the ends of the thread with a knot.

**5**  Take the threaded needle and insert it into the underside of the garment close to the edge where you want to begin attaching the trim. Pull the needle through until the knot is right up against the fabric.

**6**  Starting at the edge, begin stitching the trim onto the garment. Use a simple running stitch or whipstitch, depending on the desired effect. If using whipstitch, insert the needle through both the trim and garment fabric, pulling gently to keep the stitches even.

**7**  Continue stitching along the entire length of the trim, making sure to keep it taut but not overly stretched. Adjust the pins as you go along to ensure the trim remains in place.

**8**  Once you reach the end of the trim, secure the stitching by sewing several small stitches close together. Knot the thread on the underside of the garment and trim any excess thread.

**Finishing touches:**

**9**  Carefully remove the pins from the trim, ensuring that it is securely attached to the edge of the garment.

**10**  Give the garment a final check for any loose threads or inconsistencies before wearing or styling it as desired. Ensure that the trim is even and lies flat against the fabric. Make any necessary adjustments by re-stitching or smoothing out the trim.

# Adding
*a waist*

Adding an elasticated waist is a relatively simple process and one that is a game changer when shopping vintage. Have you fallen in love with a dress that's too big? Do you have a jacket that's no longer flattering? Adding a cinched-in waist can automatically turn this piece from oversized to tailored for you!

## Things You'll Need

- **Clothing to be upcycled**
- **Air- or water-soluble marker or chalk**
- **Measuring tape**
- **Additional fabric for a channel**
- **Scissors**
- **Iron and ironing board**
- **Pins**
- **Sewing machine or hand sewing needle**
- **Thread in coordinating colour**
- **Elastic (your waist size plus a bit extra for comfort. I recommend that the elastic isn't too thin so it holds as much fabric as possible)**
- **Safety pin**

## Technique

**Prepare the item and elastic:**

1   Before starting, make sure the garment is clean and ready to work on.

2   Put on the garment inside out, or on a friend or mannequin to determine where you want your elasticated waist to sit. You can either use your natural waistline or go for a higher or lower waistline, depending on your preference.

3   With an air- or water-soluble marker or chalk, mark the waistline all around the garment. If it doesn't have a clear waistline, you can measure and mark it at regular intervals.

4   Measure your waist size and add a bit extra for comfort. Cut the elastic to this length and attach a safety pin to one end. This will help you thread the elastic through the channel.

**Cut and sew the channel:**

**5** With your scrap fabric, cut a strip of fabric for the channel the length of the waistline and a bit wider than the elastic, plus extra for seam allowances all round. Fold the seam allowance to the wrong side all around and press in place. Place the channel along the marked waistline and pin in place, making sure the fabric doesn't slip.

**Tip:** To make a feature of this upcycle if you are confident in your sewing ability, you can make the channel in a contrast fabric and sew it on the outside of the garment, rather than sewing on the inside – see the image on page 48.

**6** Using a sewing machine or needle and thread, sew a straight line close to each long folded edge to create the channel, leaving the short ends open to insert the elastic. Make sure to backstitch at the beginning and end for added durability.

**Tip:** These instructions are for adding an elastic waistband to a dress. If you are working on a garment like a jacket, you obviously won't want to join the ends of the elastic together. Instead, stitch the elastic to the garment at each end of the channel to secure it after checking the fit in step 7.

If you are only doing this for a part of your garment as I have done here, simply pin the ends of the elastic at each end of the channel, and secure them with a stitch at either end.

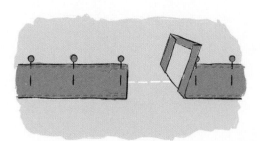

**Add the elastic:**

**7** Use the safety pin that you attached to the elastic in step 4 to thread the elastic through the channel. Gently push, guiding the pin and elastic through the entire channel until it comes out the other end. Once the elastic is threaded through the channel, safety pin the ends of the elastic together and try on the garment. Adjust the elastic to your desired waist size by pulling it tighter or letting it out slightly. Make sure it's comfortable but not too loose.

**8** Once you're satisfied with the fit, overlap the two ends of the elastic by about 2.5 cm (1 in). Pin them together to hold in place temporarily.

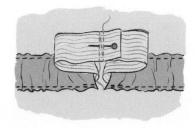

**9** Using a sewing machine, sew a few lines of straight stitches back and forth over the overlapped ends of the elastic. This will securely attach them together. Trim any excess elastic and loose threads and make sure everything is neatly finished. And there you have it! Your item now has a new elasticated waist with a channel. Enjoy wearing your newly modified garment!

# Sweater
*to vest*

Ultimate cottagecore clothing, turning a sweater into a vest or sleeveless tunic is a fun and creative way to upcycle your old and worn-out sweaters or jumpers. Follow this step-by-step guide to transform your favourite knitwear into a stylish vest.

## Things You'll Need

- **Old jumper/sweater**
- **Measuring tape or ruler**
- **Marking chalk or pencil**
- **Fabric scissors**
- **Sewing machine and/or overlocker (serger)**
- **Thread in coordinating colour**
- **Pins**

## Technique

**Prepare the sweater:**

1   Decide on the look you want for your vest. Try on your sweater and determine where you want the shoulders to end (and the armhole to start and end) – do you want it cropped and tight, or loose and oversized? You should also mark where you want the hem to be.

2   Lay your sweater flat on the workspace, making sure it is evenly stretched out and the front and back align.

3   Using a measuring tape or ruler, find your marking for where you want the vest to end, and measure from the bottom hem of the sweater up to this point, marking this length all along the bottom, ensuring it is straight and even. Leave 1.5 cm (⅝ in) extra to hem the bottom. Or you can leave the hem as it is if you like the current length.

## Cut the pieces:

**4** Carefully cut along the marked lines, removing the bottom portion of the sweater to create the desired vest length. If you have an overlocker (serger), overlock (serge) this edge to stop the knit unravelling, but if not you can use a zigzag stitch on your sewing machine. Remember to use caution when cutting and sewing to avoid any accidents!

**5** You'll need to mark out your new armhole position, and remove the sleeves. I like to keep this as close to the original armhole as possible to ensure the fit is correct.

Remember, you need leave 1.5 cm (⅝ in) extra for the hem of the armhole. Measure and mark the new armhole from your earlier markings. Make sure the marks are symmetrical on both sides. Cut along the marked lines to create the armholes. Be cautious while cutting to ensure you do not accidentally cut through both layers of the sweater. If you have an overlocker, overlock this edge to stop the knit unravelling, but if not you can use a zigzag stitch on your sewing machine.

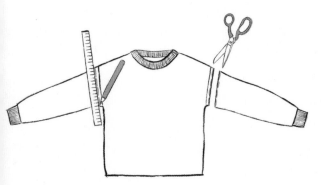

## Stitch and finish:

**6** Fold about 1.5 cm (⅝ in) of the armholes and bottom edge towards the inner side of the vest, creating a clean hem. Use pins to secure the folded edges in place.

**Note:** you are not double folding the hems because you do not want to create too much bulk, depending on the thickness of your knit.

**7** Using a sewing machine, carefully sew along the pinned hemlines to secure them. Sewing a straight line along the edge will give a neat and finished look.

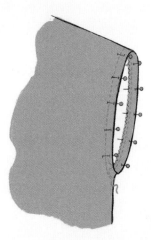

**8** Inspect your finished vest and trim any loose threads. Give it a press with an iron if needed. Your transformed sweater to vest is ready to wear and enjoy!

Balaclava

Influenced by the need to mask up during the global pandemic, these little accessories have become the new fave winter warmer and the cutest accessory!

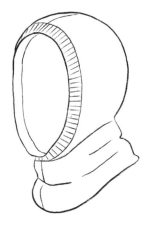

## Things You'll Need

- **Old knitted piece (I suggest a sweater or blanket)**
- **Pattern**
- **Chalk or air- or water-soluble marker**
- **Scissors**
- **Sewing machine and/or overlocker (serger)**
- **Thread in coordinating colour**
- **Pins or clips**
- **Loop turner or a chopstick/ metal straw if you're making the optional drawstring**
- **Steam iron and ironing board**
- **Safety pin**

**Tip:** If you are cutting your balaclava from a chunky knit, and you want to have a drawstring, it's best to use a length of cord or piping for this, as you knit will just be too thick to make a practical drawstring.

Scan QR code to download the pattern for this project

## Technique

**Prepare the pieces:**

1    Lay the sweater or blanket on a flat surface and flip it inside out. As it's knitted, make sure it's not twisted or folded. Take a fabric marking pen or chalk and carefully trace the outline of the pattern pieces onto the wrong side of the item. Be as accurate as possible, and don't forget to transfer the additional pattern markings because it will be harder to do so later. If at all possible, place the front of the balaclava (the opening) along the bottom of the sweater or edge of the blanket so it doesn't unravel, as shown in the illustration below.

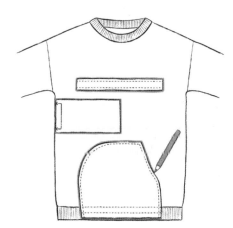

**2** With a pair of sharp scissors, cut out the pattern pieces. Take your time and make precise cuts to ensure a clean and professional result. If you have an overlocker (serger), overlock (serge) all raw edges to prevent them from unravelling. If not, use the zigzag stitch on your sewing machine to finish the edges.

### Begin sewing:

**3** Place the two sides of the hood right sides together, and stitch down the centre seam of the hood from the top front, around the outer curve, to the back neck.

If you want a drawstring, at each position A along the opening of the hood, use a zigzag or buttonhole setting on your machine to stitch a circle or rectangle. This will be what you pull the drawstring through. You then need to create a channel along the opening hood of the balaclava so that it's adjustable to wear. To do this, fold over the edge of the hood by 3 cm (1¼ in) to the wrong side and stitch along this line. Be aware this will be visible on the outside, so either use a matching thread, or use a contrast thread if you want to add a little detail.

**4** Then take your neck piece, and with right sides together, pin the longest side (the width) to the bottom of the hood. Using your sewing machine and a stretch stitch, stitch along this line so you now have what looks like more of a balaclava shape (see the illustration below). Complete this shape by stitching both ends of the neck piece right sides together down the centre-front seam.

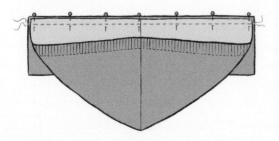

**5** Fold the bottom edge inward by about 1 cm (⅜ in) and pin it down. Stitch along this line using a sewing machine or by hand with a needle and thread. This step is not necessary if you prefer a raw, edgy look.

### Add the drawstring and finish up:

**6** Join the drawstring strips along one short end with right sides together. Press the seam open then fold the strip in half, right sides together, and sew along the long edge, and one end, then trim the excess from the seam allowances. Turn the fabric tube right side out through the open end using a loop turner. If you don't have a loop turner, use a long blunt object (like a chopstick or metal straw). When the drawstring is right side out, use a blunt object to push out the corners and edges for a clean finish. Make sure the fabric is completely turned right side out and the seam is centred and give it a press.

**7** Pin the safety pin to one end of the drawstring and thread into one end of the channel. Gently push, guiding the pin and drawstring through the entire channel until it comes out the other end. Knot each end of the drawstring to be sure it can't slide back through the channel. Carefully turn the balaclava right side out and smooth out any wrinkles or folds if necessary. Slide the balaclava over your head to check the results, and make any further adjustments to match your desired fit and comfort level. You're finished! Remember to set the new shape with a steam iron.

Patchwork
Dad shirt

Dad shirts are in themselves an amazing thrifted item for both quality and volume of fabric available second-hand! They're cool, but jazzing them up a bit can take them from your boyfriend's wardrobe to high-end fashion. You can go from mixing up just a few panels to full patchwork. Here's how.

## Things You'll Need

- **Shirts to patchwork**
- **Seam ripper**
- **Measuring tape**
- **Air- or water-soluble marker or chalk**
- **Sharp scissors**
- **Iron and ironing board**
- **Pins or clips**
- **Sewing machine**
- **Thread in coordinating colour**

## Technique

**Prepare the item and plan the design:**

1   Find some shirts at least two to three sizes larger than your current size so they're long enough – check they cover your bum before beginning!! Try to make sure all the shirts are the same or similar sizes.

2   Lay out the shirts on a clean, flat surface, and decide what placement you'd like. Consider the size, shape, and colour of the patches and placement that would best complement and enhance the design of each new shirt.

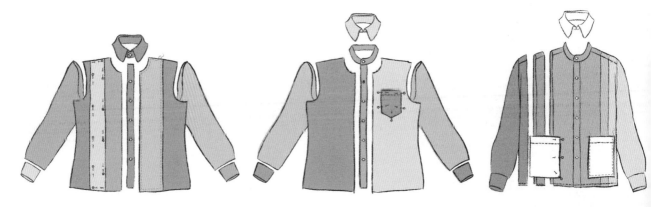

## Cut and sew the patches:

**3** Using your seam ripper, unpick the shirts. Unpick the main seams (the pocket, collar stand, side seams, front placket, armholes and cuffs) so you essentially have your pattern pieces for each shirt. You can swap the pieces around and decide on a new layout by eye, or use one of my suggestions. If you also want to add patches, choose one of the shirts to cut into squares/rectangles to make your patches from. Fold all patch edges in by 0.5 cm (¼ in) and press them down, so that the edges are not frayed.

**Tip:** Be careful not to cut into the seam allowance on the shirt pieces – that's why it's best to use a seam ripper rather than scissors.

**4** If you are not adding patches, go straight to step 5. Place any patches on the main shirt according to your design plan, using pins to secure them temporarily in position. This will prevent any shifting while sewing. Sew each patch in place all around the edge using small, even stitches either by hand or on your sewing machine, making sure that the stitches catch the patch. You can either use a simple straight stitch, or if you want to be more edgy you could even use a zigzag stitch. Remove the pins carefully.

## Assemble and finish:

**5** It's best to go seam by seam so as to not get confused here! Start with the shoulder seams, as shown in the illustration above right, then the armholes, the cuffs, then the placket, and finally the collar. Temporarily pin the seams in place with the right sides together. This is why it's best to have the same-size shirts, as then the seams will naturally match up. Secure each piece in place with a straight stitch on your sewing machine. Once the seam is complete, give it a press so it's nice and neat.

**Tip:** If you have different size shirts, you will have to go with the smaller size length the hem, and cut away the extra material from the larger shirt(s).

**6** Trim any excess threads and inspect the patches for loose threads or areas that may require touch-ups. Press the shirts with an iron to smooth out any wrinkles and reveal the final patchwork design. I hope you love it!

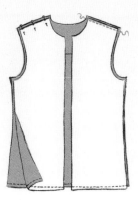

### Did you know...

Second-hand clothes have a hugely positive social and environmental impact. They reduce carbon emissions, and save lots of resources, water, and energy. They also prevent old clothing from ending up in landfills or incinerators. Plus they cost less, and who doesn't like a good deal, right? Not only does buying used reduce the number of natural resources being used, it also reduces the amount of energy used and pollution that's being emitted by things like pesticides, burning fuel in the trucks that haul the items, toxic chemicals and carbon emissions.

# Tablecloth
*to dress*

If you are used to traditional sewing, a tablecloth is a fantastic stretch of fabric to be turned into... anything! The great thing about this project is that you can use this pattern for a shorter or longer dress depending on the size of the tablecloth.

## Things You'll Need

- **Pattern**
- **Tablecloth (preferably 100% cotton)**
- **Measuring tape or ruler**
- **Air- or water-soluble marker or chalk**
- **Scissors**
- **Sewing machine and/or overlocker (serger)**
- **Thread in coordinating colour**
- **Pins**
- **Bias binding in complementary colour**
- **Iron**

| Finished measurements | | XS | S | M | L | XL |
|---|---|---|---|---|---|---|
| Length | (cm) | 130.6 | 131.3 | 132 | 132.7 | 133.4 |
| | (in) | 51½ | 51¾ | 52 | 52¼ | 52½ |
| Bust | (cm) | 98 | 104 | 110 | 116 | 122 |
| | (in) | 38½ | 41 | 43¼ | 45¾ | 48 |
| Waist | (cm) | 100 | 106 | 112 | 118 | 124 |
| | (in) | 39¼ | 41¾ | 44 | 46½ | 48¾ |
| Sleeve | (cm) | 55.1 | 55.7 | 56.3 | 56.9 | 57.5 |
| | (in) | 21¾ | 22 | 22¼ | 22½ | 22⅝ |

Scan QR code to download the pattern for this project

## Technique

**Plan and cut the pattern:**

1  Lay the tablecloth out on a flat surface and decide which part will be the top and the bottom of the dress. Print and prepare your pattern pieces and pin them to the fabric. See how much of the dress will fit on your fabric. Use the cutting line for the short sleeves if you need to and you can leave off the ruffle too – you could even crop the dress to make a top!

   **Tip**: If you have a beautiful detail like a scalloped edge or embroidery, think about where you could use this. The scalloped edges would look fab as the hem, and embroidery tends to look great on the bodice, framing the neckline, but each placement will be different depending on the tablecloth.

2  With a pair of sharp scissors, cut out the pattern pieces. Cut carefully, ensuring that both sides of the dress are symmetrical.

**Begin sewing:**

3  Sew up the shoulder seams. You can either overlock (serge) the edges so that the seams don't fray, or if you are more confident in sewing, you can French seam them instead!

4  Bias bind the neckline with a complementary colour. To do this, open out the bias binding along one side and pin the raw edge along the raw edge of the neckline with right sides together, allowing a little extra at the start of the binding to turn under, and positioning it so the ends of the binding will overlap at one shoulder seam (see the illustration on page 68). Sew around the neckline in the fold line of the binding, cut away the excess fabric and fold the bias binding over the raw edges to enclose them and cover the seam. Sew the other edge of the binding down with a straight stitch along the edge. If you don't want to see the bias binding, you can turn it inward and stitch is down along the neckline. At this point, try on

## How to French seam

Sewing a French seam is a wonderful way to achieve a clean and professional finish. Start by placing the fabric pieces *wrong* sides together and sewing a narrow seam allowance, around 0.5 cm (¼ in) from the edge. Trim down this seam allowance to around half the width, and press it towards one side. Now, fold the fabric right sides together, enclosing the trimmed seam allowance within this new fold. Sew another seam, approximately 0.5 cm (¼ in) away from the folded edge, enclosing the raw edge within the seam. Carefully press this seam flat. Check there are no frayed edges poking out from the seam (if so give them a trim) and you are left with a durable and tidy finish on the inside of your project.

the bodice and determine if the waistline is where you want it to be. If it isn't, you can cut away the length not needed evenly from the edge.

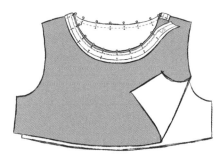

5    Run gathering stitches along the top edge of each sleeves and gather to fit the armhole (see page 17). Line up the centre of the sleeve to the shoulder seam, and pin it in place with the gathers evenly distributed. Then stitch this seam in place with a straight stitch. Fold the bottom edge of the sleeves inward by 1 cm (⅜ in) twice, to hide the raw edges. Then straight stitch to hold the hem in place.

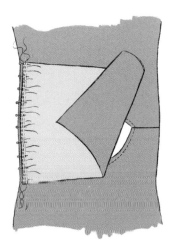

6    With the right sides of the fabric facing each other, pin the two side edges of the bodice together and continue pinning along the sleeve underarm seam. Use a straight stitch to sew these two seams. Repeat to sew the side seams of the two skirt pieces and skirt ruffle.

7    You will need to gather across the top edge of the skirt pieces. Sew two parallel gathering stitches along the top edge with a long stitch, 0.5 cm (¼ in) from the edge (within the seam allowance), so that you can evenly gather the edge. Once you have made the gathers, pin the skirt piece in place to the bottom of your bodice, adjusting the gathers slightly to ensure they are even and fit this width. Stitch the skirt in place with a straight stitch and remove the pins. Trim any excess fabric and finish the edges with zigzag stitch or an overlock stitch to prevent fraying. Repeat to attach the ruffle to the bottom of the skirt.

**Finish and check fit:**

8    Try the dress on again and determine the desired length for your height. Mark the hemline with chalk or a fabric marker. Fold the bottom edge of the dress inward twice, to hide the raw edges, creating a clean finish. Pin the hem in place and sew along the folded edge.

9    Finally, try the dress on to check the fit and overall look. Make any necessary adjustments, such as taking in the sides or adjusting the length. Once you are satisfied with the fit, give the dress a final press with the iron to ensure it looks polished and neat, trim any threads, and enjoy your unique creation!

**Tip:** If you are making use of a finished edging on your tablecloth at the hem, as I did, obviously you won't need to hem it again. If you need to make the skirt or ruffle shorter, without redoing the hem, you can unpick the top, gathered seam, trim it and then reattach it.

Jeans
to skin

A denim midi is the perfect day-to-night wardrobe piece. Ranging from low-rise to high-waisted, bleach white to midnight black, and printed to distressed, the style's newfound popularity means there are plenty of upcycling options to choose from. As brands also jump on the bandwagon, why not try make your own?

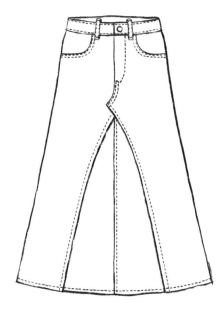

## Things You'll Need

- **Two pairs of jeans (of a similar weight, but not necessarily of the same colour depending on the look you want. Your 'pair one' will need to fit you on the waist)**
- **Seam ripper**
- **Measuring tape**
- **Air- or water- soluble marker or chalk**
- **Scissors**
- **Pins**
- **Sewing machine**
- **Thread in coordinating colour**
- **Air- or water-soluble marker or chalk**

## Technique

**Cut and prepare the pieces:**

1   With pair one, turn your jeans inside out and locate the inseams (the seams running along the inside of each leg). Using a seam ripper or scissors, carefully unpick the inseams, working from the bottom hem to the crotch. This step helps to open up the legs. Measure only 5 cm (2 in) of the crotch from the leg seam at the front only and use the seam ripper or scissors to unpick so that this area can lay flat when you are making the skirt. Repeat on the back.

2   Using scissors, cut off the legs of the second pair of jeans just below the crotch area, ensuring the cuts are straight. Cut along one side seam of these legs so that they then open out. Save one leg to use for the back of the skirt, if desired.

**Tip:** If you have an overlocker (serger), overlock (serge) the raw edges of both pairs of jeans.

**3** Lay your first pair of jeans flat on a table, right side down. Place your middle panel in between the legs. When lining the pieces up, try to match the centre seams of the jeans together. Pin along these new seams, from the bottom hem up to where the crotch begins. This will join the two legs to form the front of the skirt. If your middle panel is much longer at the top, cut away the excess material.

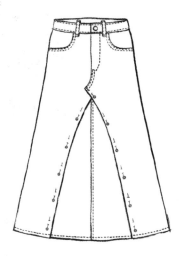

## So why upcycle denim? Did you know...

+ Levi Strauss, reports that over 3,780 litres (999 US gallons) of water are used to produce just a single pair of 501® jeans.

+ According to Oxfam, emissions produced manufacturing jeans are comparable to flying a plane around the globe 2,372 times or a petrol car travelling more than 21 billion miles.

+ Studies show that up to 20% of fabric is wasted in the production of denim clothing. Much of this waste ends up in landfills or is incinerated, contributing to greenhouse gas emissions and other environmental damage.

**Begin sewing:**

**4** Using a sewing machine, stitch along the pinned edges, removing the pins as you go. Ensure you sew a straight line, securing the fabric together.

**5** Try on your skirt. If you find the skirt is too long, you may need to adjust it. Use a measuring tape to establish the desired length. Mark any required alterations with a fabric marker.

**Tip:** If you don't like the back being open, repeat the steps on the back using the remaining leg of your second pair of jeans. Make sure you have enough space to walk if you decide to do this, as the split generally gives you room to move.

**Add a hem:**

**6** If you wish to shorten the skirt, cut off the hem, if you haven't already done so. Fold the raw edge up towards the inside of the skirt by around 1.5 cm (⅝ in). Then fold it over again, this time by about 2.5 cm (1 in), and pin it in place. Stitch along the folded edge, removing the pins as you sew. Alternatively, you can leave the skirt with a raw edge, which is also very popular now! Your two jeans transformed into a skirt are now ready, and you can enjoy wearing your upcycled creation!

Three T-shirt upcycles

# Patchwork graphic tee

The world (and me personally) has too many old T-shirts! They're endlessly available at charity and vintage shops, so here are my top three T-shirt upcycles, starting with a simple patchwork transformation.

## Things You'll Need

- **Two to three old T-shirts**
- **Air- or water-soluble marker or chalk**
- **Ruler**
- **Pins or clips**
- **Scissors**
- **Iron and ironing board**
- **Sewing machine**
- **Thread in coordinating colour**

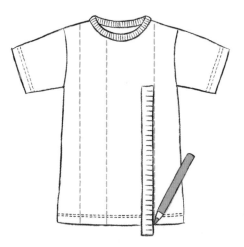

## Technique

**Prepare the T-shirts:**

1   Find two or three T-shirts that are the same size and that you think will look cool together.

2   Lay the T-shirts flat on a table or workspace. Decide which part of each shirt you want to use for your final design. It could be the front or back, or a combination of both. In this example, I have used the centre front, centre back and sleeves, but if you want to be a bit more experimental (like diagonal) go for it!

3   Use chalk or a removable marker and a ruler to mark on one of them where you are cutting your T-shirts. How you decide to cut up your t-shirts is completely up to you! You could simply cut each t-shirt in half, or split them several ways as shown opposite.

4   Stack the T-shirts with the marked T-shirt on the top. Align the edges as closely as possible. Use pins to secure them together, ensuring they do not shift during the cutting process.

5   Use scissors to cut along these lines. Once you have made the necessary cuts, remove any stray threads or loose ends. Take your iron and carefully press the cut edges to create neat and crisp lines. This step is particularly important if you are using jersey material as it tends to curl at the edges.

**Tip:** You will not need to overlock (serge) the edges because jersey doesn't fray!

6   Swap the pattern pieces you have just cut around to arrange your new placement.

**Begin sewing:**

7   Thread your sewing machine and set it to a straight stitch.

8   With right sides together, begin sewing the pieces along the cut edges, about 0.5 cm (¼ in) from the edge. Continue sewing until you have reassembled your T-shirt, ensuring you catch both layers of fabric in your stitch. Remove the pins as you sew.

**Final adjustments:**

9   Try on the newly sewn T-shirt and make any adjustments, if necessary. Take note of any areas that require additional stitching or alterations for a better fit.

10  Give your T-shirt a final pressing with the iron to smooth out any wrinkles or creases caused during the sewing process. Finally, don't throw away the other parts of your T-shirts. Use them to create another patchwork T-shirt or to make pockets for other garments, perhaps.

## Did you know...

Fifteen million discarded T-shirts a month are shipped to Ghana alone, and 40% of that ends up being burned, put into the ocean or dumped in a landfill! On average, the carbon footprint of a single T-shirt is 5.5 kg (121 lb) CO2e (carbon dioxide equivalent), with the largest impact coming from production (MADE-BY, 2012). By repairing and maintaining your clothes, you avoid the need to purchase new ones, thus reducing the carbon emissions associated with their production and transportation

# Balloon-sleeve crop top

If you've got a couple of plain boring T-shirts, you can give one a major makeover by using the other one to make some stylish sleeves. I've used two T-shirts in the same colour, but if you don't mind contrast sleeves then you can use any combo you like!

## Things You'll Need

- **Two T-shirts**
- **Air- or water-soluble marker or chalk**
- **Ruler**
- **Pins or clips**
- **Scissors**
- **Iron and ironing board**
- **Sewing machine**
- **Thread in coordinating colour**
- **Elastic (enough to go round both arms where you want the bottom of the sleeve to sit)**
- **Safety pin (optional)**

## Technique

**Prepare the T-shirts:**

1   Find two T-shirts that are two sizes larger than your size and the same colour.

   **Tip:** Sometimes I will use old discoloured white T-shirts and dye them together.

2   Try one of the T-shirts on. Mark with a removable marker where you want to crop it.

3   Lay the T-shirts apart, flat on a table or workspace. Use a ruler to draw a line where you want to crop the main T-shirt. Draw another line 3 cm (1¼ in) lower for your hemline. This is where you are going to cut.

**4** On this T-shirt use fabric scissors to cut along the line you just made, and cut off both sleeves. Take your iron and carefully press the cut edges to create neat and crisp lines. This step is particularly important if you are using jersey material as it tends to curl at the edges but you will not need to overlock (serge) these edges as jersey doesn't fray.

**5** On the other T-shirt, cut off the original hem. Draw two lines with a removable marker, one 15 cm (6 in), and one 30 cm (12 in) up from the bottom of the T-shirt for your sleeves. Cut along these two lines as they are your new sleeves.

**Begin sewing:**

**6** Work gathering stitches along the top of both sleeve pieces (see page 17).

**7** Next, pin the sleeves to the original armholes, trying to make the gathers even. Use stretch stitch, if you have one, to sew the sleeves in place, removing the pins as you go.

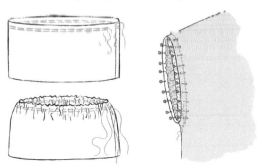

**8** At the bottom of your sleeves, fold the edge up by 2 cm (¾ in) to create a channel. Iron and pin this fold in place. Then stitch as close to the edge of the 2 cm (¾ in) fold as possible, leaving a small opening to insert the elastic.

**Add the elastic and finish off:**

**9** Pin a safety pin to the end of one piece of elastic and feed it through the channel on one sleeve. Try the T-shirt on to make sure it feels comfortable. Tie the elastic ends together, and sew up the opening on the sleeve. Repeat to add elastic to the other sleeve.

**10** To hem the bottom of your T-shirt, turn up the bottom edge by 1.5 cm (⅝ in), iron and pin in place. Stitch the hem to finish.

**11** Give your T-shirt a final pressing with the iron to smooth out any wrinkles or creases caused during the sewing process and trim off any loose threads.

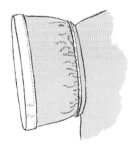

# Halterneck crop top

Who knew that you could take one large T-shirt and turn it into something so sexy? What's more, this top is fully lined and can be assembled in two ways, either to cross in front of the neck or as a standard halter-neck, depending on what suits your style.

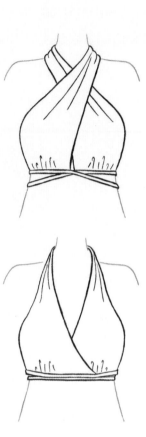

## Additional items needed

- **One XXL T-shirt**
- **Halter-neck pattern**
- **Pins or clips**
- **Scissors**
- **Iron and ironing board**
- **Sewing machine**
- **Thread in coordinating colour**

Scan QR code to download the pattern for this project

## Technique

**Prepare the T-shirt:**

1   Lay your T-shirt on a table or workspace. Use chalk or an erasable marker and a ruler to mark where you are cutting by following the pattern pieces.

2   Lay out your four triangular front pieces. Sew two of the front pieces together along the small centre-back seam. Repeat this on the other pair, so you have two long pieces.

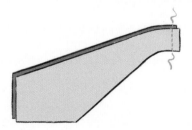

**Begin sewing:**

**3** Lay the two pairs of joined front pieces right sides together on top of each other, and pin around both long curved outer seams. Sew these two seams with a straight stitch, removing the pins as you go.

**4** Turn this long tube right side out through the gap on either of the side seams. This is the front and neck of the crop top. Position the two front pieces with one overlapping the other , as shown in the illustration above, or with the two long front edges meeting in the middle, depending on how you want to wear your top.

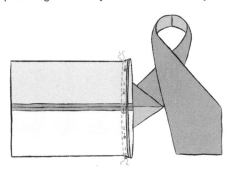

**5** Sew the two rectangles with right sides together along one of the longer seams. This is your bodice.

**6** Pin the front halter-neck piece to your bodice with right sides together. Match the short side seam edges of the back bodice to the side seams of the halter-neck front pieces– they should be the same length. You will have to unfold both pieces to do this, and sew them so that you can't see this seam from the outside.

**7** Press the seams and lay the top flat.

**8** Stitch a long gathering straight stitch along the bottom edge of the bodice across the front area and as close to the edge as possible so that it can be hidden in the seam when the tie piece is added. Gather the area.

**Make the tie and finish up:**

**9** Finish with the bottom tie. Stitch the two tie pieces together at one end to make one very long tie piece.

**10** Pin this piece to the bodice back with right sides together, aligning the centre seam you have just sewn to the centre back of the top. Then continue to pin the tie all the way to the front.

**11** Stitch the tie down 0.5 cm (¼ in) from the edge, sewing through both layers of the bodice..

**12** Fold the tie over twice, to encase the raw edges at the bottom of the halter-neck. Pin this down, and stitch along the tie, as close to the edge as possible to secure.

**13** Give your new top a final pressing with the iron to smooth out any wrinkles or creases caused during the sewing process. Trim off any loose ends, and you're finished!

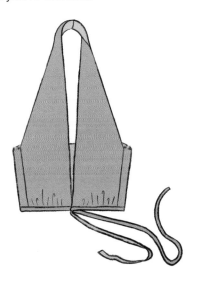

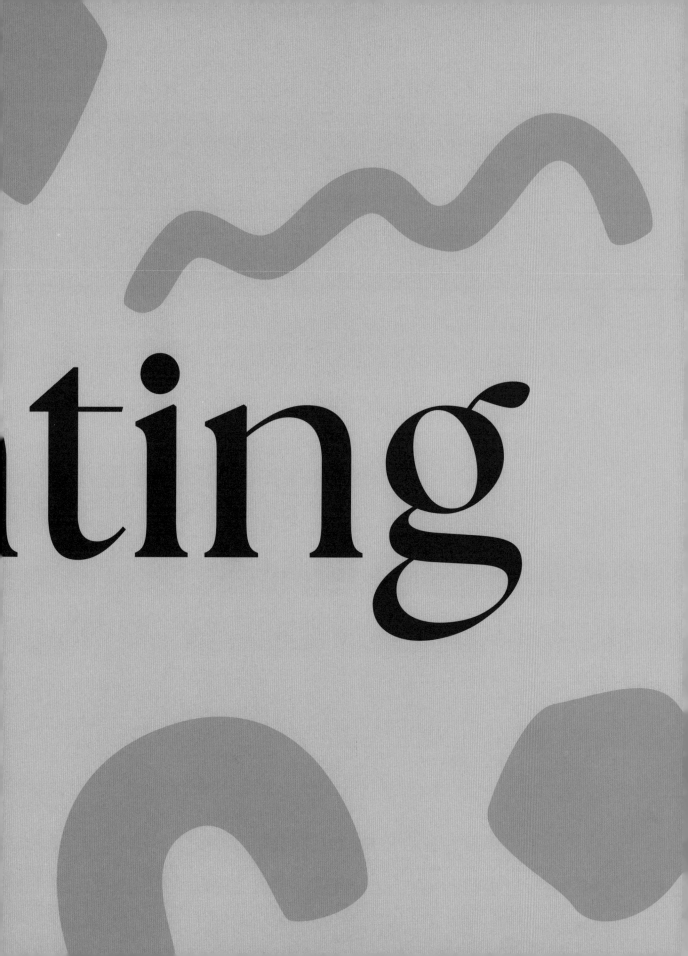

Scrunchie

*p92*

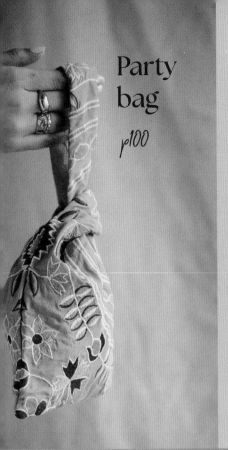

Party
bag

*p100*

Tote bag *p102*

Hair
bow

*p96*

# Waistcoat
*p112*

# Collar
*p108*

Patchwork
quilt *p118*

Quilted
jacket *p124*

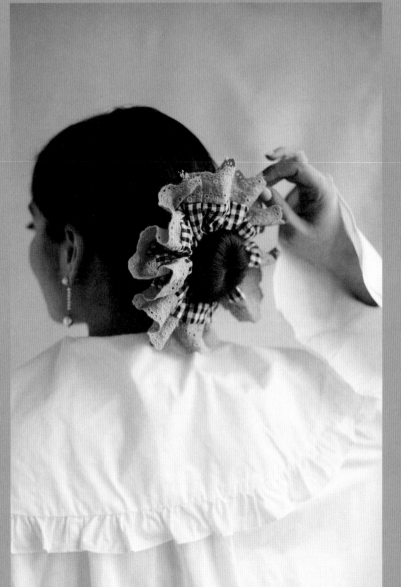

# Scrunchie

A scrunchie is my go-to accessory to add a bit of flavour to any outfit, so I thought it's only right to make it our first creation together. It only takes one scrap of fabric (and maybe a fancy trim if you like it) so let's get started. Remember, you can personalize your scrunchie by using different fabrics, patterns, or added embellishments like bows. Enjoy wearing or gifting your handmade scrunchie!

## Things You'll Need

- Scrap fabric minimum 10 x 56 cm (4 x 22 in)
- Measuring tape/ruler
- Scissors
- Pins
- Sewing machine or hand sewing needle
- Thread in coordinating colour
- Elastic 1 cm (⅜ in) wide and approximately 23–25 cm (9–10 in) long
- Safety pin

## Technique

**Prepare the pieces:**

1   Choose your fabric from your bundle of scraps, and cut it into a strip. The standard measurement for a scrunchie is 56 cm (22 in) long and 7.5–10 cm (3–4 in) wide. However, you can adjust the length and width according to your preference (I like them wide!). Fold the fabric in half lengthwise, with right sides together.

**2** Then pin the edges together along the short sides to create a loop of fabric, making sure to leave a small opening of about 2.5 cm (1 in) in the middle for turning the scrunchie right side out later.

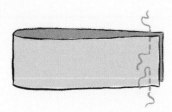

**3** Press 1 cm (⅜ in) over to the wrong side on both long edges.

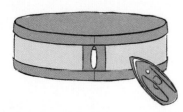

**4** Pin the long edges together, with the pressed seams enclosed in the tube. If you have any fun additional trims, such as the pink lace I used on my scrunchy, you can also enclose them here.

**Begin sewing:**

**5** Sew along the pinned long side using a straight stitch on your sewing machine. If hand sewing, use a running stitch. Start sewing as close to the edge as possible for neatness. Continue sewing until you reach back to the beginning, then backstitch to secure the seam.

**6** Trim any loose threads and carefully remove the pins.

**Add the elastic and finish up:**

**7** Measure the elastic by wrapping it around your wrist and adding about adding 1.5 cm (⅝ in) overlap. I use between 5–7.5 cm (2–3 in) elastic. Cut the elastic.

**8** Attach a safety pin to one end of the elastic and insert it through the gap in the fabric tube. Keep the other end of the elastic secure, so it doesn't get pulled into the tube.

**9** Once the elastic is fully inserted, overlap the two ends by about 2.5 cm (1 in) and pin them together.

**10** Sew the elastic ends together securely using a zigzag stitch on your sewing machine or by hand sewing. Make sure to reinforce the stitch by sewing back and forth a few times.

**11** Push the elastic inside the tube, ensuring it is evenly distributed along the scrunchie. Stitch the small opening closed by hand or using a narrow straight stitch on your machine.

**12** Trim any loose threads, and your scrunchie is complete!

Hair
*bow*

One reason for the resurgence of hair bows could be the popularity of vintage fashion. Bows were a staple accessory in the 1950s and '60s, and as the perfect hair-down update, it's no surprise that they're making a comeback. Experiment with different fabric choices, sizes, and shapes to create unique bows for various projects or occasions.

## Things You'll Need

- **Scrap fabric minimum 20 x 10 cm (8 x 4 in)**
- **Measuring tape**
- **Scissors**
- **Iron and ironing board**
- **Pins**
- **Sewing machine**
- **Thread in coordinating colour**
- **Hand-sewing needle**

## Technique

**Prepare the fabric:**

1  Choose the fabric for your bow – you can use two contrasting or matching fabrics, depending on your preference. Cut two rectangular pieces of fabric. The size of the rectangles will depend on the desired size of your bow. As a general guideline, a rectangle measuring around 20 x 10 cm (8 x 4 in) works well for a medium-sized bow. You will also need a narrow strip of fabric for the centre wrap and tails, approximately 5 cm (2 in) wide and twice the length of your bow. In my example, I actually went even longer for dramatic affect at around 8 x 80 cm (3¼ x 31½ in).

2  If your fabric is wrinkled, it's a good idea to iron it before sewing. This will ensure a neater finish. Set your iron to the appropriate temperature for the fabric you're using and carefully iron out any wrinkles or creases.

3  Place the fabric rectangles for the bow on top of each other, right sides together. Pin them together to secure.

**Begin sewing:**

4   Using a sewing machine, sew all the way around the pinned fabric rectangles. Use a straight stitch and a 0.5-cm (¼-in) seam allowance. Start sewing in the middle of one of the long edges, and when you get all the way round, leave a gap of about 2 cm (¾ in). Repeat this step for the centre wrap.

5   Trim the excess fabric close to the sewn edge, leaving a small seam allowance. Be careful not to cut into the seam, but ensure you cut across the corners as well for a neater finish when the fabric is turned out. Once trimmed, carefully turn the fabric right side out. Use a blunt object, such as a pencil or chopstick, to push out the corners for a crisp appearance.

6   If desired, you can use an iron to press the fabric bow. This step is optional but can help achieve a smoother and more polished look. Set your iron to the appropriate temperature for the fabric and gently press the bow.

**Finish the bow and add the centre wrap:**

7   Hand stitch your small opening closed with a hand sewing needle. Pinch the centre tightly, which will create folds, transforming your rectangle into a bow shape. Use a pin to secure the folds temporarily.

8   To finish your bow, you now need to add the centre wrap. Wrap the strip around the centre of the pinched bow, covering the seam. Secure the strip with a few stitches by hand or using the sewing machine. Cut away any final loose threads. If you have made your strip longer, allow the ends to hang loose as the tails of your bow.

9   You can attach the bow to a garment or accessory by simply sewing. Sew through the back of the bow, attaching it securely to your desired item like a hairclip or a shirt. Congratulations and enjoy your chic new bow!

## Styling Tip:

A bow is a fabulous accessory to add to a hair clip or slide, but you could also go wild and make 20 to add to a jumper, down the side of some trousers or to accessorize a bag! The possibilities are endless.

# Party
*bag*

Japanese knot bags, also known as 'mochi' or 'kinchaku' bags, originated in Japan and have been used for centuries. Traditionally they were made from kimono fabric scraps and were used to carry various items, such as personal belongings, money, craft supplies, or small gifts. Over time, Japanese knot bags gained popularity around the world due to their versatility and minimalist aesthetics, and in the right materials can be the cutest party bags – think fluffy, sparkly or even faux fur for that ultimate party bag!

The dimensions of our finished knot bag will be around 20 x 40 cm (7⅛ x 15¾ in). Your pattern has a 1 cm (⅜ in) seam allowance.

## Things You'll Need

- **Fabric of your choice (preferably two contrasting fabrics)**
- **Fusible interfacing (optional)**
- **Pattern**
- **Air- or water-soluble marker or chalk**
- **Scissors**
- **Pins or clips**
- **Sewing machine**
- **Thread in coordinating colour**
- **Iron and ironing board**
- **Hand sewing needle**

## Technique

**Choose and prepare the fabric:**

1   Japanese knot bags are traditionally made using two contrasting fabrics, so have a look through your scraps and select fabrics that you like and that complement each other well. You can alternatively use the same fabric throughout for a modern twist. Make sure to wash and iron the pieces beforehand for best results. Add fusible interfacing if your fabric needs more structure.

2   Fold your fabrics in half and cut the pattern through both layers from each fabric.

Scan QR code to download the pattern for this project

**Begin sewing:**

**3** Keep your cut pieces in pairs, right sides together, and secure in place with pins or clips. Start stitching, beginning just below one handle, and go along the bottom edge, all the way to the other side, as shown in the illustration below. Stop stitching below the second handle. Stitch across the upper edge of each handle. Repeat the entire process with the second set of fabric pieces.

**4** Cut across the seam allowances at the corners to reduce bulk. Turn one of the fabric pieces right side out. Insert it into the second piece.

**5** Align the two bags with each other and secure everything in place with pins or clips. Don't connect all four layers together! Keep the gap between the two sets as marked on the pattern, or you'll end up sewing the bag shut.

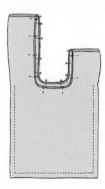

**6** Sew around the curve between the handles. Make some shallow cuts along the inside curve of the handle to ensure the curved seam is neat when you turn it the right way out. Turn the entire knot bag right side out through one opening at the handle.

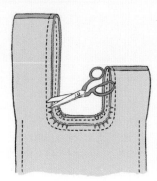

**Finishing:**

**7** Now you will need to topstitch along the inside curve between the handles. Start stitching at the top seam of one handle and sew all the way round.

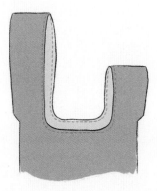

**8** All that's left is to finish the outer edges of each handle that are still raw and unstitched. Press the seam allowances to the inside along these edges and pin the openings closed. Hand stitch the openings closed to finish.

**9** Press the bag to emphasize its crisp lines.

# Tote bag

One of the easiest and quickest makes, it's a no-brainer! The environmental effect of single-use plastic bags has been widely publicised, which has in turn meant that reusable tote bags have become hugely popular. Tote bags are a great environmentally friendly solution for those looking to reduce their environmental impact.

**Final measurements**
33 x 38 cm (13 x 15 in)

adjust sizing for a different size tote

## Things You'll Need

- **Fabric (cotton is best)**
- **Optional: fabric for lining**
- **Measuring tape or ruler**
- **Air- or water-soluble marker or chalk**
- **Scissors or rotary cutter**
- **Pins**
- **Sewing machine**
- **Thread in coordinating colour**
- **Iron and ironing board**

## Technique

**Cut and prepare the pieces:**

1   Using the measuring tape or ruler, measure and cut two rectangles of your outer fabric 34.5 cm (13½ in) wide by 39.5 cm (15½ in) high (this includes a 1.5 cm (⅝ in) seam allowance). If you wish to line the bag, repeat with your lining fabric.

2   Measure and cut two fabric strips for the bag handles. The length depends on how long you want them to be, typically 50–65 cm (19¾–25½ in), and the width around 5–7.5 cm (2–3 in) plus a 1.5 cm (⅝ in) seam allowance on all edges.

3   Fold each fabric strip in half lengthwise, with right sides together. Pin the long edges together and then sew, leaving the short ends open. Turn the fabric right side out and press the handles with an iron to make them flat and neat. For a neater finish, overlock (serge) or zigzag stitch the ends of the handles.

**Begin sewing:**

4  Pin the two outer fabric rectangles right sides together and stitch down the sides and across the bottom edge. If you are lining your bag, repeat the process, but this time leave a gap of about 10 cm (4 in) in one side seam, as shown in the illustration.

5  Optional: to create a boxed corner, take one bottom corner of the bag and fold it flat so the side seam lies over the bottom seam. Measure and mark a perpendicular line at a distance from the corner, depending on how wide you want the base of the tote bag to be (typically 2.5–5 cm/1–2 in). Pin and sew along the marked line, securing the boxed corner. Trim the excess fabric, leaving a small seam allowance. Repeat for the opposite corner of the tote bag and also for the lining, if applicable.

6  If you aren't going to line the bag, turn a hem along the top edge, then pin the handles to the inside of the bag, spacing them symmetrically. Sew the handles securely by sewing a rectangle shape with an X inside it.

**Add the lining:**

7  If you have made a lining, pin the handles to the bag, with right sides facing, matching the ends of the handles to the top of the bag and placing them symmetrically. Tack (baste) to secure them, then place the lining fabric and the outer fabric right sides together, making sure the handle loops are pointing down and sandwiched between the layers. Sew along the top edge. Trim the seam allowance, and turn the bag right side out through the opening. Press the top edge with an iron, making sure it looks neat. Hand stitch or machine stitch the opening closed in the lining.

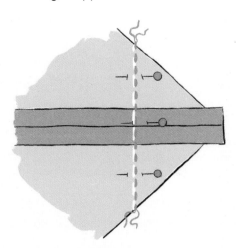

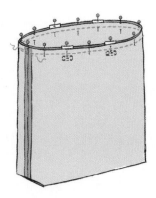

Collar

These oversized collars deserve to be part of your new-season look, and are a great size to make use of your old scrap fabrics. A fun yet elegant trend, you can pair a shirt and pretty Peter Pan collar with a shirt, jeans and your favourite trainers for an off-duty look, or you could opt for a fitted cocktail dress with Peter Pan detailing for your next soirée.

## Things You'll Need

- **Fabric (cotton or any other lightweight material)**
- **Pattern**
- **Iron-on interfacing**
- **Air- or water-soluble marker or chalk**
- **Scissors**
- **Pins**
- **Sewing machine or needle and thread**
- **Thread in coordinating colour**
- **Knitting needle or other blunt-tip item**
- **Iron and ironing board**
- **Measuring tape or ruler**
- **Bias binding in complementary colour**

## Technique

**Prepare and cut the collar pieces:**

1   Fold your two pieces of fabric in half. Place the pattern to the folded edge of both fabrics, and trace your template with chalk. You can always shape the collar differently by redrawing the bottom curve as desired. Cut along the marked curve through both layers of fabric. For a crisp finish, iron interfacing onto one collar piece.

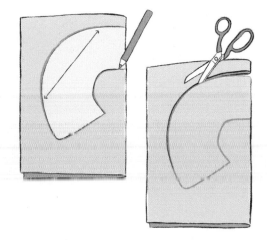

Scan QR code to download the pattern for this project

**2** If you want to add a ruffle to the outer edge of the collar, cut these four pieces as well. Cut the ties from the fabric if you don't want to use the collar binding as the ties.

**Begin sewing:**

**3** Place two of the ruffle pieces right sides together and sew across one short end. Press the seam open. Repeat with the second two pieces. Place the assembled pieces right sides together and sew around three sides, leaving one long edge open. Turn the ruffle strip right sides out, press and then gather along the open edge to fit the outer edge of the collar.

**4** Now we're going to start with the collar. Pin and stitch the centre back seams on the main fabric and the lining and press. Pin the collar and lining together around the outer edge. If you are adding a ruffle or other trim, first pin the trim, right sides together, to one collar piece, all round the outer collar curve, matching the raw edges. Pin the second collar piece right sides together on top so the ruffle is sandwiched in the middle. If you are not adding a ruffle, simply pin the two collars right sides together. Now sew around the outer curve, taking a 1 cm (⅜ in) seam allowance. Backstitch at the beginning and end to secure the stitches.

**5** Trim any excess fabric from the seam allowances to help prevent any bulk in the seams. Make small, straight clips around the curves without cutting through the stitches. This makes the seam much neater when you turn it right side out.

**6** Reach inside the collar and gently pull it through the opening, turning it right side out. Use a blunt object, like a knitting needle, to carefully push out the corners of the collar ends for a smoother shape.

**7** Lay the collar flat on an ironing board and press it gently with an iron to remove any creases.

**Add the binding and finish up:**

**8** Measure the neckline and cut the binding to match with an additional 30 cm (12 in) at each end if you want to use this as your ties. Open out the bias binding along one side and pin the raw edge along the raw edge of the neckline, matching the centre of the binding to the centre-back neck edge of the collar. Sew around the neckline in the fold line of the binding, backstitching at the beginning and end to secure the stitches. Trim the seam allowance to neaten it.

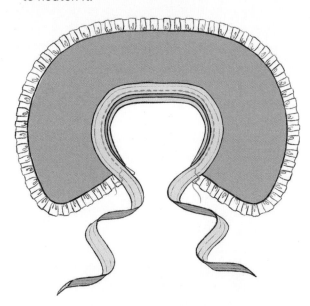

**9** Fold the binding over the raw edge of the neckline to enclose it. Starting at one end of the binding, stitch the binding, around the neckline curve and all the way to the ends. You now have a collar with ties that you can do up in a bow at the front when you wear it.

**10** Trim any excess threads. Give the collar a final press with an iron to make it lay flat and look polished. Your detachable Peter Pan collar is now ready to wear with any garment you like!

Waistcoat

The most perfect transitional piece from season to season, this popular style is timeless and looks flattering on every body shape. Practical, but also super chic, it's a must-have in your wardrobe.

## Things You'll Need

- **Waistcoat pattern**
- **Fabric (preferably quilted, or fabric plus wadding/batting and lining)**
- **Pins**
- **Sewing machine**
- **Thread in coordinating colour**
- **Scissors**
- **Measuring tape**
- **Iron**
- **Bias binding**

| Finished measurements | | XS | S | M | L | XL |
|---|---|---|---|---|---|---|
| Length | (cm) | 55 | 55.4 | 55.8 | 56.2 | 56.6 |
| | (in) | 21½ | 23¾ | 22 | 22⅛ | 22¼ |
| Bust | (cm) | 98 | 104 | 109 | 115 | 121 |
| | (in) | 38⅝ | 41 | 42⅞ | 45¼ | 47⅝ |
| Centre back to hem | (cm) | 53 | 54.5 | 56 | 57.5 | 59 |
| | (in) | 20¾ | 21½ | 22 | 22½ | 23¼ |

Scan QR code to download the pattern for this project

# Technique

**1**  Wash and iron the fabrics to remove any wrinkles or sizing – if you are quilting your own fabric, you should do this after you have quilted the layers. If you are not using a quilted fabric, you will need to quilt it first. Place the fabric right side down, add the wadding on top, then layer the lining fabric. Pin the layers together. Using your sewing machine, quilt the layers following your desired quilting pattern. You can create straight lines, diagonal lines, or any pattern you like. Trim any excess wadding or fabric that may be sticking out.

**2**  Now that your fabric is prepared, cut out your pieces using the pattern provided. Make sure you refer to the finished measurements for the best fit. Your pattern has a 1 cm (⅜ in) seam allowance.

**Begin sewing:**

**3**  Place the back and front pieces right sides together and pin along the sides and shoulder seams. Sew along the pinned edges with a straight stitch. Trim the seam allowance, clipping any curves or corners. Turn the waistcoat right side out and press the seams with your iron to flatten them. If you are making your waistcoat reversible, you will need to add bias binding to this seam. If not you can simply overlock this seam to keep it neat.

**4**  Leave the top edge of the pockets, and focus on adding binding to the other three edges. Open out one edge of the bias binding and sew with right sides together around the other three sides of the pocket. Fold the binding over to the inside to enclose the raw edge and stitch in place. If you are not using bias binding, simply fold over these edges ready to be topstitched. Then fold and press the seam allowance on the top edge of each pocket piece. Topstitch in place. Pin the pockets in position on the front of the waistcoat. The positioning is marked on your pattern. Sew around three sides of each pocket, leaving the top edge open. You can use a decorative stitch if desired.

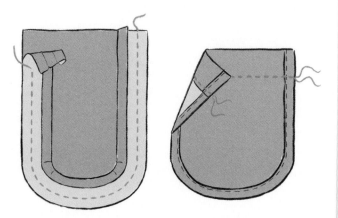

**Add the binding:**

5    I like to start at the centre-back neck, as the
     start can be tricky! Open out the bias binding
     and fold over one raw end to get a clean
     edge. Start by applying the bias binding on
     the right side, pinning and stitching as you go,
     around the whole of the outside edge, from the
     neckline, down the front and along the bottom,
     then on round until you get back to the start.
     Overlap the starting end slightly. Once you have
     finished, press the bias binding seam to ensure
     the edge is neat. Trim the seam allowance in
     half and clip any curves or corners. Then fold
     over the binding to enclose the seam allowance.
     Pin in place, and topstitch the binding down.
     Remember, this stitch will be seen, so try to
     ensure it is as neat as possible!

6    Sew the bias binding to the armholes of the vest
     in the same way. They can be a little tricky, as
     they are on a curve, so make sure you take your
     time, pinning and pressing as you go.

7    Optional: If you are adding ties, fold the long
     strips in half with right sides together and stitch
     along both long edges and one end. Turn right
     side out. Pin the ties to the waistcoat and stitch
     as marked on the pattern. Press the waistcoat
     with an iron, ensuring the seams are neat and
     flat. As another alternative, you can make your
     ties from leftover binding.

Patchwork quilt

Typically a sentimental gift, or a family keepsake, why not make a quilt with this fun patchwork design! A quilt is typically three layers – the top, which is decorative, the wadding (batting), which is an insulating layer, and the backing, which hides the construction – all held together with quilt stitching through all layers. Cut it from something sentimental for a loved one, or use your favourite scraps to update your bedroom. Remember, practice makes perfect when it comes to quilting, so don't get discouraged if your first few attempts aren't perfect. Keep trying, have fun, and enjoy the process of creating your own beautiful quilt!

**Final measurements**
170 x 170 cm
(66⅞ x 66⅞ in)

## Things You'll Need

- **Pattern**
- **Fabric scraps for patchwork top**
- **Ruler**
- **Air- or water-soluble marker or chalk**
- **Scissors/rotary cutter**
- **Sewing machine**
- **Thread in coordinating colour**
- **Iron and ironing board**
- **Wadding (batting)**
- **Backing fabric**
- **Quilting pins**
- **Quilting needles**

Scan QR code to download the pattern for this project

# Technique

## Measure and cut the pieces:

**1**  Use the table below and the sizes on the pattern to cut the pieces for your quilt top. Remember this includes a 0.5 cm (¼ in) seam allowance on all sides.

| Small Square | White | 41 |
|---|---|---|
| | Colour 1 Pink | 4 |
| | Colour 2 Blue | 6 |
| | Colour 3 Green | 10 |
| Triangles | Colour 4 Amber | 36 |
| | Colour 1 Pink | 46 |
| | Colour 2 Blue | 36 |
| | Colour 3 Green | 46 |
| | White | 80 |
| Large Square | White | 20 |

**2**  Take the cut fabric pieces and lay them out on a flat surface to create the quilt-top design. If you are not following the colour guide but using different pattern fabrics, play around with the arrangement until you are happy with the overall look.

## Begin sewing:

**3**  Start sewing the fabric pieces together to create the quilt top. Place two pieces of fabric right sides together and sew a 0.5 cm (¼ in) seam along one side using your sewing machine. First join the triangles to the edges of the small squares to create large squares. Then you can join the large squares into rows. After sewing each seam, press it open with an iron. This will ensure a neat and flat finish.

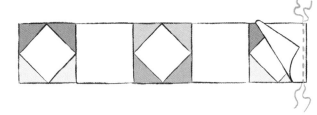

**4**  Keep this process going until you have completed every row, then join the rows to finish.

**5**  Cut your backing fabric and wadding to the same size as your quilt top.

**Tip:** Adhesive wadding massively helps here if you are a beginner, so that it doesn't slip.

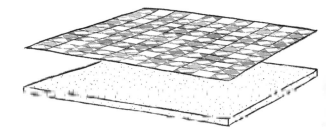

## Why is using sustainable materials so important?

Use materials that are environmentally friendly, such as organic cotton, recycled fabrics, and biodegradable alternatives to synthetic fibres. Synthetic textile fibres are produced from fossil-fuel resources, such as oil and natural gas. Their production, consumption and related waste-handling generate greenhouse-gas emissions, use non-renewable resources and can release microplastics.

**Quilt the layers together:**

6   Place your quilt top on the wadding (batting), right side up. Pin the layers together using quilting pins to secure them in place. If you are using adhesive wadding, you can simply iron the layers together, but if not stitch them together, by stitching in the ditch (along the seam lines) to keep the layers together and keep the wadding evenly distributed. For ease, simply sew in vertical and horizontal lines.

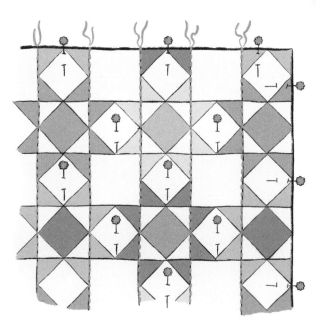

7   Once you have finished quilting, trim off any excess fabric and wadding around the edges of the quilt.

**Add the backing and finish up:**

**8** Place the backing fabric on top of your quilt, right sides together. Pin around the entire edge of your quilt and sew a straight stitch around the edge, leaving a 10 cm (4 in) gap at the bottom to turn it the right way out.

**9** Cut away the seam allowances at the corners to ensure they are nice and neat when turned the right way, and turn the quilt the right side out. Make sure all the corners are neatly pushed out with a blunt object.

**10** Handstitch the opening shut with a needle and thread, and cut away any loose trims.

**11** You can now complete your final quilt design trough all three layers. Choose a quilting design that you like (for example vertical lines every 5 cm (2 in), or a more exciting design you can draw with chalk freehand. Sew slowly and carefully to ensure even stitches. Give your quilt a final press with an iron, and it's ready to use or display!

**Tip:** You can use this technique to make your fabric for future projects, like the quilted jacket hack!

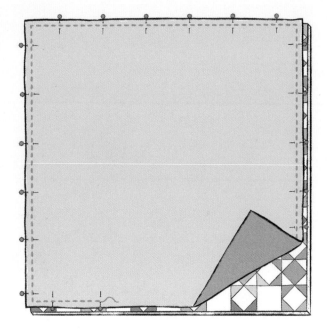

Quilted jacket

Upcycled coats and jackets made from quilts are an internet sensation, and I'm obsessed. The fashion girlies rocking these beauties are making a case for some maximalist fun and I am here for it! Any type of bedding you can actually wear outside the bedroom is a winner in my book.

## Things You'll Need

- An old quilt or fabric scraps for patchwork top
- Ruler
- Air- or water-soluble marker or chalk
- Scissors/rotary cutter
- Sewing machine
- Thread in coordinating colour
- Iron and ironing board
- Wadding (batting)
- Quilting pins
- Quilting needles
- Pattern
- Bias binding in complementary colour

| Finished measurements | | XS | S | M | L | XL |
|---|---|---|---|---|---|---|
| Length | (cm) | 69.5 | 70 | 70.5 | 71.5 | 72.5 |
| | (in) | 27⅜ | 27½ | 27¾ | 28⅛ | 28½ |
| Bust | (cm) | 125 | 129 | 132 | 136 | 141 |
| | (in) | 49¼ | 50¾ | 52 | 53½ | 55½ |
| Waist | (cm) | 130 | 135 | 141 | 146 | 151 |
| | (in) | 51⅛ | 53⅛ | 55½ | 57½ | 59½ |
| Sleeve | (cm) | 56 | 56.5 | 57 | 57.5 | 58 |
| | (in) | 22 | 22¼ | 22½ | 22⅝ | 22⅞ |

Scan QR code to download the pattern for this project

# Technique

## Prepare the fabric and cut the pieces:

**1** Follow steps 1–6 on pages 120–122 to make your quilted fabric and cut out your pattern pieces.

## Assemble the jacket:

**2** Begin by sewing the shoulder seams of the front and back panels right sides together, using a straight stitch. Press open the seams using an iron.

**3** Attach the sleeves into the armholes by pinning them with right sides together, aligning the notches of the sleeve and armhole. Stitch along the armhole curve, ensuring the sleeve is evenly distributed. Sew the side seams of the jacket from the bottom hem to the end of the sleeve, again with right sides facing. Press open these seams as well.

**Tip:** To make a matching collar follow the instructions on pages 108–111.

## Attach the bias binding:

**4** To finish off the edges, add bias binding around the outer edge of the jacket. Start at the centre back neck, as the start can be tricky. Open out the bias binding and fold over one raw end to get a clean edge.

**5** Start by applying the bias binding on the right side, pinning and stitching as you go, around the whole of the outside edge, from the neckline, down the front, along the bottom, then round until you get back to the start. Overlap the start slightly. Once you have finished, press the bias binding seam to ensure the edge is neat. Trim the seam allowance in half and clip any curves or corners. Then fold over the binding to enclose the seam allowance. Pin in place, and topstitch the binding down. Remember, this stitch will be seen, so try to ensure it is as neat as possible!

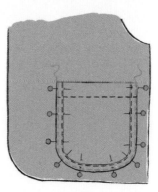

## Add the pockets:

**6** Attach binding to the sides and lower edge of each pocket in the same way as before. If you are not using binding, simply fold over the edges ready to be topstitched. Then fold and press the seam allowance on the top edge of each pocket piece to the wrong side. Topstitch in place. Pin the pockets on the front of the jacket, following the positioning on your pattern. Sew around each pocket, leaving the top edge open; use a decorative stitch if desired.

**Tip:** Line the centre backs together when adding the collar to ensure it is in the correct position.

## Finishing touches:

**7** Secure any loose threads and give the jacket one last press to ensure a professional finish.

# Buttons

Sometimes all it takes is a button refresh to update that new shirt jacket! Or perhaps you still love a pair of jeans but the buttonhole is ripped!. Here's how to replace or reattach a button, and fix a buttonhole!

## Things You'll Need

- **Garment to mend or refresh**
- **Small scissors**
- **Hand sewing needle**
- **Thread in coordinating colour**
- **Patch (optional)**
- **Button if required**

## Technique to fix a buttonhole

**Preparation:**

1. Examine the buttonhole and identify any issues, such as loose threads, fraying, or a completely ripped hole. If the buttonhole has loose threads, carefully trim them using small scissors. Be careful not to damage the fabric.

2. If the buttonhole is completely torn, you can reinforce it by applying an iron-on patch, or stitching a small denim square behind the area. You can then follow step 3 to reinforce the ripped area.

**Begin sewing:**

3. Depending on the amount of damage to the buttonhole, you may be able to save it just by working backstitch around it, as shown in the illustration. If it's really bad, you can darn the surrounding area and work buttonhole stitch around the buttonhole – there are lots of videos online to show you how. Stitch along the edge of the buttonhole, creating small, close together stitches. Repeat this process on the opposite side of the buttonhole. Continue stitching until you reach the other end of the buttonhole and secure the thread with a knot on the wrong side of the fabric. Trim any excess thread.

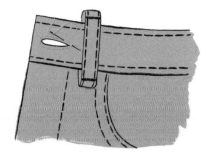

# Technique to replace a button

## Preparation:

1   Before starting, check if there is a spare button on the inside of the garment, or if not source a button that matches both the size and colour of the original button.

    If you are changing the buttons for a clothing update, why not make something of them with a colour clash or a fun design.

2   Using a small pair of scissors, carefully remove the threads that held the original button in place. Be careful not to cut or damage the fabric.

3   Make sure the needle is double threaded with a knot at the end. Insert the needle from the wrong side of the fabric, coming out through one of the button's holes.

## Begin sewing:

4   Keeping the button slightly away from the fabric surface (a matchstick or similar between button and fabric is good for this), insert the needle through one of the opposite holes on the button. Push the needle through the fabric to the back again. Repeat this process a few times, working through all the button's holes in turn, ensuring the button is securely attached.

5   Before fastening off, bring the needle up to the surface of the fabric underneath the button and wind the thread around the strands under the button a few times. This creates a shank under the button to allow for the thickness of the fabric around the buttonhole.

6   Take the needle back down to the wrong side again and make a few small stitches to secure the thread, then cut off the end.

# Darning a hole in knitwear

Restore your favourite knits by fixing the hole that's been stopping you from wearing it with darning! Darning a knitted hole is a simple process that involves weaving a patch of yarn into the hole to repair it. You can make a feature of this by using a contrast yarn, blend it in by colour matching the yarn completely.

## Things You'll Need

- Knitted item to mend
- Yarn in a similar weight to the yarn in the knit
- Small scissors
- Darning needle
- Knitting or darning egg (optional)

## Technique

**Preparation:**

1   Locate the hole on your favourite knit and cut a length of yarn. Make sure the yarn matches the thickness of the original yarn as closely as possible.

2   If you have a knitting or darning egg, place it inside the garment behind the hole. The egg helps create tension and support while you work, making the darning process easier. However, if you don't have an one of these, you can still proceed without it.

3   Thread one end of the yarn through the eye of the darning needle, leaving a tail of 10–15 cm (4–6 in). Knot the tail end to prevent it from slipping through the knitwear.

**Begin darning:**

**4** Start weaving the needle and yarn through the knitwear, focusing on making small stitches around the edges surrounding the hole. Insert the needle under the adjacent stitches, being careful not to pull the yarn too tight, as it may distort the knitted stitches.

**5** Now begin weaving the needle and yarn across the hole, forming parallel rows until the hole is fully covered. Make sure to maintain an even tension to avoid distorting the fabric.

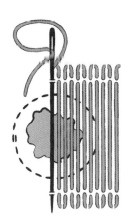

**6** Now work at 90 degrees to the first rows, weaving the needle and yarn under and over alternate strands. Again, make sure not to pull too tight and distort the fabric.

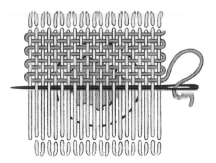

**7** Once the hole is completely covered, weave the needle under a row of stitches along the edge of the hole. This step helps secure the yarn and prevents unravelling.

**Finish up:**

**8** Carefully trim any excess yarn, leaving a small tail. Ensure that the tail is not too short, as it may unravel over time. Tuck the tail back through the knitted stitches using the darning needle.

**9** Give the repaired area a gentle stretch to help the new darning blend better with the surrounding knit. Block the area if necessary to help the newly darned hole blend in by using steam over the area. To steam block: lay your knit out on a flat surface (like a bed or towel), and pin into the shape you want. Turn your iron or steamer to the wool setting. Hold the iron/ steamer around 4–7.5 cm (1½–3 in) above your piece and steam it.

## Did you know...

Extending the lifespan of a garment by just nine months can reduce its environmental impact by 20–30% (WRAP, 2017). By taking care of your clothes and using them for longer, you can significantly reduce the carbon, water, and waste footprints associated with their production, transportation, and disposal.

# Fixing a hole in jeans

Remember, practice makes perfect, so don't worry if your first attempt is not flawless. With time and experience, you'll master the art of patching up your jeans creatively.

## Things You'll Need

- Jeans/item to mend
- Fabric patch or scrap denim
- Scissors
- Sewing needle of a sewing machine
- Thread in coordinating colour
- Pins or safety pin
- Optional: decorative embroidery thread

## Technique

**Assess the damage and prepare the patch:**

1   Take a close look at the hole in your jeans to determine its size and location. You can zigzag or overlock (serge) the edges if you wish so the patch lasts longer.

2   If you have a fabric patch or scrap denim, cut it to a suitable size, making sure it is slightly larger than the hole. This will provide enough material to securely fix the damaged area.

3   Thread the sewing needle with the thread you've chosen, making a knot at the end of the thread. Ensure the thread length is sufficient to sew around the entire hole.

   **Tip**: If you want to make the patch to look less visible, choose a matching denim colour and matching thread. If you want to make a feature of the patch, choose a contrast denim, or even a patterned fabric!

4   Place the patch behind the hole, making sure it completely covers the damaged area. This will be the foundation of your repair. To make sure it doesn't move as you are stitching, you could use pins or a safety pin to secure it.

**Begin the repair:**

5    Bring the needle through the denim from the inside, right beside the hole, and guide it through the patch

6    Using a zigzag stitch, sew around the edges of the hole, securing the patch to the jeans. Keep the stitches close together for added durability. Continue sewing around the edges of the hole in a zigzag pattern until you've reached the other end of the patch. This ensures the hole is adequately repaired and minimizes the likelihood of further fraying.

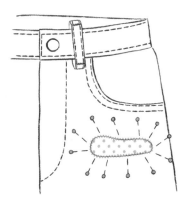

7    For added reinforcement, sew a second row of stitches around the hole, just inside the first row of zigzags. This is optional, but provides additional strength and minimizes the chance of the hole reappearing.

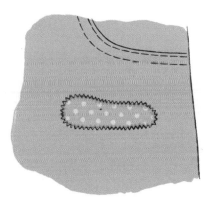

**Finish up:**

8    Trim any excess thread and secure any loose ends by tying small knots. This will prevent the repair from unravelling.

9    Optional step: get creative! You could make a feature of the repair by adding some sashiko stitching, which is lines of small running stitches usually in white thread. You can do this with embroidery thread, and find some fun templates to copy online to make the mend even more fun!

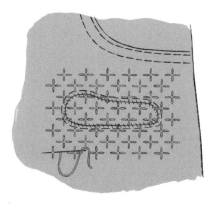

10   Finally, turn the jeans inside out and iron over the repaired area to set the stitches. This will help ensure the longevity of the repair.

# Repairing topstitching

The topstitching on your jeans is highly visible, so to keep your jeans looking fresh and to ensure they last a long time, fix any breaks in the topstitching as soon as you can to restore their original appearance.

## Things You'll Need

- **Jeans to mend**
- **Seam ripper**
- **Small scissors**
- **Hand sewing needle**
- **Thread in colour of existing topstitching**
- **Iron and ironing board**

## Technique

**Assess the damage and prepare:**

1   Identify the areas where the topstitching needs repair. Look for loose or broken stitches, or areas where the stitches have been completely ripped out.

2   Use a seam ripper to carefully remove the damaged stitches. Take your time and be gentle to avoid damaging the fabric further. Pay close attention to any loose threads and cut them off using scissors.

3   Cut a length of thread to match the topstitching and thread it through the sewing needle. Make sure to double the thread for added strength.

## What is circular fashion?

Circular fashion is a sustainable approach to the fashion industry that aims to eliminate waste and minimize the environmental impact of clothing production and consumption. It emphasizes the need to keep resources in use for as long as possible and to regenerate new materials from existing ones. Circular fashion focuses on reducing, reusing, recycling, and repairing clothing, as well as designing products with longevity and durability in mind. It encourages the use of sustainable and renewable materials, promotes ethical manufacturing processes, and encourages consumers to adopt responsible purchasing habits. Circular fashion strives to create a closed-loop system in which products are continuously recycled and repurposed, leading to a more sustainable and eco-friendly fashion industry.

**Begin sewing:**

4    Begin stitching at one end of the area that needs repair. Insert the needle from the wrong side of the fabric and pull the thread through until the knot catches. Align the fabric edges if necessary and start sewing.

5    To ensure durability, use backstitch. Bring the needle up through the fabric a short distance in front of the last stitch, then bring it back again to the point where the last stitch ended. Repeat this process for each stitch, creating a continuous line of stitches.

6    Try to match the stitch length of the existing topstitching for a seamless repair. If you can see the previous holes from the thread, use these as your guide. If you're having trouble, use a ruler, pencil, or tailor's chalk to mark the stitch length on the fabric as a guide. This will make the repair look seamless!

7    When you have reached the end of the area that needs repair, secure the thread by creating a small knot on the wrong side of the fabric, then cut off any excess thread.

**Final inspection:**

8    Inspect your repaired topstitching to ensure it matches the original. If needed, you can press the area with an iron on low heat to flatten the stitches and blend them with the fabric.

# Fixing a zip

The MOST common repair I get asked about is fixing a zip (zipper). It can be so frustrating when you have a favourite zip-up jumper and then BOOM... the zip has gone! Here's how to bring them back to life in just a few simple steps. Remember to handle zips carefully, applying only gentle force when necessary, to avoid causing further damage.

## Things You'll Need

- **Garment with damaged zip**
- **Sewing machine**
- **Needle and thread**
- **Thread in coordinating colour**
- **Pliers**
- **Seam ripper**
- **A replacement zip, if needed**

## Technique

**Identify the problem:**

1   First, carefully examine the zip to identify the problem. Look for any tangles, debris, or misalignment of the teeth. This will help you understand the exact issue and find the appropriate solution.

2   If you notice any dirt, fabric, or other debris stuck in the teeth, use a small brush or toothbrush to gently remove it. Be careful not to damage the zip or put excessive pressure on it, which may damage it further.

3   Sometimes a zip can get stuck due to lack of lubrication. Apply a lubricant suitable for zips, such as graphite powder or silicone spray or use a special zip-release spray, along both sides of the zip teeth. Move the slider up and down a few times to distribute the lubricant evenly.

## Resolve problems with the teeth or slider:

**4**   If the zip is misaligned, use your fingers or a pair of small pliers to gently align the teeth back into position. Ensure that the individual teeth on each side interlock correctly.

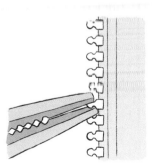

**5**   If the slider is stuck in one position and won't move at the bottom of the zip, you can create a new zip stop by simply sewing over the zip just above the missing teeth to prevent the slider from reaching the damaged section and slipping off – but make sure you can still get the garment on and off if you do this!

**6**   If the slider is damaged or broken, you will need to replace it. You can purchase a new slider that matches the size and style of your zip online or from a craft/sewing shop. Remove the old slider by using pliers to gently squeeze and separate it from the zip teeth. Slide the new slider onto the teeth, aligning them properly, and ensure it moves smoothly up and down the track. (You can actually find some really fun sliders online!)

**Tip:** There are many different zips used dependent on the weight of the fabric (for instance, denim will have a heavier zip compared to a light cotton). You will need to match the zip exactly to replace the slider or to repair missing teeth.

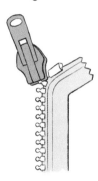

**7**   If you notice that some of the zip teeth are missing, you can attempt to repair them. Using a needle and thread, fill in the gaps by attaching a new fabric or zip tape, ensuring it is aligned correctly with the surrounding teeth.

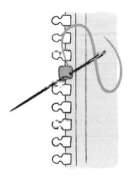

**Replace the zip:**

8  If all attempts to fix the zip fail or it is severely damaged, you may need to replace the entire zip. Measure the length of the damaged zip from the top of the top stop to the bottom of the bottom stop and purchase a replacement online, or from a craft/sewing shore. Carefully remove the old zip by unpicking the stitches attaching it to the fabric.

9  Attach the new zip by sewing it along the seam or where the old zip was originally placed. Ensure that the zip teeth align with the fabric correctly and test its functionality before finishing the sewing. You can find step by step instructions on sewing a zip on page 18. If the zip is in a difficult place, like below a waistband, you may have to unpick further to release the zip and sew in the new one. If this is the case, use your seam ripper to do so, and then follow the instructions on pages 139–140 to complete the waistband once the zip has been replaced.

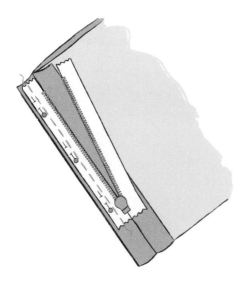

## Did you know...

Repairing clothes reduces the demand for new ones, decreasing the need for production. According to the Ellen MacArthur Foundation, if the average utilization of clothing (the number of times a garment is worn) was increased by just 20%, it could lead to a 3% reduction in carbon, water, and waste footprints associated with the clothing industry.

# Repairing stressed/ split seams

Your most loved garments are often the first ones to show signs of wear, sometimes in embarrassing places, such as the seat of your jeans. Before things get any worse, dig out a needle and thread to make a repair.

## Things You'll Need

- **Garment to mend**
- **Fusible interfacing or iron-on patch (optional)**
- **Iron and ironing board**
- **Sewing machine or hand sewing needle**
- **Thread in coordinating colour**
- **Pins**

## Technique

**Identify the problem and prepare for the repair:**

1   Start by assessing the split or stressed seam. Determine the extent of the damage and identify the areas that need repair.

2   Make sure both the garment and patch fabrics are clean. If the edge of the fabric (where you sew) is frayed or has holes, you will need to use a backing to strengthen the fabric here. You can either use a fusible interfacing, or an iron-on patch to do this.

3   You can use your sewing machine, or a hand sewing needle, with a matching thread colour to the fabric. If you are using a hand sewing needle, knot the end of the thread to secure it. This will prevent the thread from pulling through the fabric while you sew.

4   Gently pull the fabric together, aligning the split or stressed seam as closely as possible. Hold it in place, using pins to ensure it doesn't move as you sew.

**Begin the repair:**

5   Begin stitching from the inside of the fabric, so the knot is hidden and doesn't show on the finished side. Insert the needle through one side of the fabric, pulling the thread until the knot sits flush against the fabric. If you are hand sewing, create a small stitch by inserting the needle back through the fabric, directly opposite to the initial insertion point. Ensure you catch both layers of fabric as you sew. If you are using a machine, use a small stitch to ensure it holds well.

6   Keep creating regular small stitches along the seam, pulling the thread taut but not overly tight. Keep the stitches close together to ensure a strong repair.

7   When you reach the end of the split or stressed seam, make a few small stitches to secure the thread in place, then cut the excess thread close to the fabric. If you are using a machine, use a backstitch to ensure it is secure.

8   To strengthen the repair further, you can sew another row of stitches directly next to the initial row. This will create a double-stitched seam and add more durability.

**Finishing:**

9   Inspect the seam repair to ensure it is secure and the fabric is aligned properly. If any loose threads remain, trim them carefully.

# Repairing a hem

Are your trousers always too long and getting scuffed on the floor? Here's how to take them up, and repair that damaged hem. By following these steps, you should have them looking as good as new!

## Things You'll Need

- **Garment with damaged or too-long hem**
- **Pins or clips**
- **Air- or water-soluble marker or chalk**
- **Seam ripper or small scissors**
- **Hand sewing needle**
- **Thread in coordinating colour**
- **Iron and ironing board**

## Technique

**Mark the hem and prepare to sew:**

1   If you are shortening your trousers, start by either unpicking the current stitching to fix immediately or take the opportunity to shorten the hem at the same time. Try on the trousers and determine the desired length: use a mirror or ask someone to help you ensure the length is even on both legs. Fold the excess fabric up to the desired length and pin or clip in place.

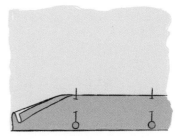

2   Once you have determined the correct length, use an erasable marker or chalk to mark the new line all around both legs. Make sure to remove the trousers and lay them flat on a table or ironing board for easier measurements.

**3** If you have a damaged hem, remove the marking pins and any existing thread or tacking (basting) stitches from the original hem. You can use a seam ripper or small scissors for this

**4** Fold the excess fabric up, aligning it with the marked hemline. Make sure the fold is even and straight all the way around the trousers. If you are shortening the trousers significantly, cut away some of the excess fabric. Fold the raw edge under a second time and use pins or clips to secure the hem in place. This will ensure that the fabric doesn't move while you're sewing.

**5** Put on the trousers to check if the hem is at the desired length and even all around! Make any necessary adjustments if needed.

**6** Cut a length of thread that is roughly double the length of the hem. Insert one end of the thread through the eye of the needle and pull it through until both ends are equal in length.

### Begin the repair:
**7** Starting from the inside of the trousers, push the needle up through the upper folded edge of the hem. Pull the thread through until a short tail is left on the inside.

**8** Working with small, even stitches, sew along the fold using a hemming stitch. Make sure to catch a few threads of the trousers in each stitch to secure the fold. Continue sewing until you reach the starting point.

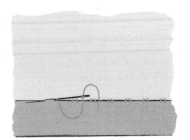

**9** To secure the stitching, create a knot at the end of your thread. Take a small stitch and loop the thread through the loop before pulling it tight. Repeat once or twice to create a secure knot.

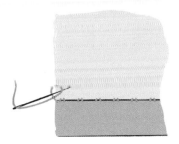

**10** Use a pair of scissors to carefully trim any excess thread. Make sure not to cut the fabric itself.

### Press your new hems:
**11** After finishing the stitching, iron the hem with a pressing cloth or directly using low heat to make it look neat and crisp.

# Dyeing fabric

So you have your best shirt or blouse, and there's a huge stain on the collar. What do you do? DYE IT! Just remember that the new colour has to be darker than the stain!

## Things You'll Need

- **Garment to dye (must be a natural fibre such as cotton, silk or wool)**
- **A natural dye, or a packet dye**
- **Gloves**
- **Stainless-steel bowl or bucket large enough to immerse the item completely**
- **Old towel or plastic sheet**
- **Plastic spoon**

In the image opposite from top left to bottom right: turmeric, cochineal, logwood, madder and weld.

## Technique

**Prepare the garment and select the dye:**

1   Identify the garment you want to dye, ensuring it is made of a fabric suitable for dyeing. Buy the appropriate fabric dye in a colour of your choice, or see A Guide to Natural Dyes on page 155 if considering a natural dye. If you do use a packet dye, be sure to check the instructions.

2   Examine the garment for any stains, loose threads, or areas that need repair. Address these issues before dyeing, as the dye can make imperfections more noticeable. Wash the garment thoroughly, without using fabric softener. This helps remove any dirt or chemicals that may affect the dye absorption.

**Prepare the dye:**

3   If using a natural dye, see How to Use Natural Dyes on page 154. If using a packet dye, read the manufacturer's instructions on the dye package carefully. Most dyes require combining the dye powder or liquid with warm water. Wearing gloves, mix the dye according to the instructions in the bowl or bucket, ensuring it dissolves completely.

If desired, dilute the dye by adding more water for a lighter shade or increase the dye's intensity by adding more powder or dye concentration.

4   Choose a well ventilated space to dye your garment since some dyes may release fumes. Cover any surfaces you don't want to stain or use an old towel or plastic sheet to protect your work area. Place the bucket or basin of dye in your work area.

**Dye the garment:**

5   Wet the garment thoroughly in warm water; this ensures even dye absorption. Submerge the garment completely into the dye bath, using a gentle stirring or swirling motion to ensure even colour distribution. Continue stirring or agitating the garment in the dye bath for the recommended duration mentioned in the dye package instructions. This can range from a few minutes to several hours. Check the garment's colour periodically by removing it from the dye bath and rinsing it under cool water until the water runs clear. This allows you to gauge the dye's intensity and decide if you want to continue dyeing.

6   Rinse the dyed garment in cool water until the water runs clear, ensuring all excess dye is removed. Fill a sink or basin with warm water and add a small amount of gentle detergent. Gently agitate the garment in the soapy water to cleanse away any remaining dye. Rinse the garment again in cool water to remove the detergent thoroughly.

7   Finally, hang the garment to air dry or follow the care instructions on the fabric label for appropriate drying methods. Enjoy wearing your new, personalized creation!

## How to use natural dyes:

1   Simply chop up your desired ingredient if it isn't crushed already, and add if using leaves or roots and add it to a saucepan with enough water to fully cover it. Bring the water to a boil over medium heat and allow to simmer for one hour. Then allow the water to come to room temperature. Strain the liquid into your dye bath container.

2   To use your dyes on fabric, you'll need to set them first. This is done by applying a fixative (also called a mordant) to your fabric prior to dyeing. Salt and vinegar are both natural fixatives and a good way to go with these types of dyes, with salt being ideal for dyes made from fruits and berries and vinegar ideal for dyes made from plants. Combine either 135 g (½ cup) salt with 1920 ml (eight cups) water or equal parts vinegar and water in a saucepan, then add your fabric and simmer for one hour. Then wring out your item ready to be dyed.

3   Now add your item to the dye bath. Make sure that make sure that the fabric is completely covered by the dye solution if you want an even result. Remember, the colour will be darker when wet than dry! When you're done, run the fabric under cool water and wash gently to remove excess dye, then hang to dry.

4   To play with the end results, you can experiment with the time you use these natural dyes to change the depth of the colour. If you leave them to soak overnight for example, you're more likely to get a much richer colour. You may even want to play with modifiers to change the colours slightly, like iron (iron sulphate) and copper (copper sulphate). Iron often turns the colours greener, while copper may make the colour more reddish. You can purchase these from most natural-food stores.

# A guide to natural dyes: a colourful journey

The revival of natural dyes is gaining momentum. These amazing plant-based dyes offer a sustainable alternative to shop-bought dyes while lending a unique character to fabrics and crafts. Let's dive into the vibrant world of natural dyes and explore some of the best options available along with the colours they produce.

## Natural dyes for hand-dyeing:

+ **Madder root:** pinks, oranges and reds
+ **Turmeric:** yellows and oranges
+ **Weld:** olive green and yellows
+ **Chochineal:** pinks
+ **Logwood:** blues, purples and blacks
+ **Indigo**

## Madder root:

Derived from the roots of the *Rubia tinctorum* plant, it produces colours ranging from pale pinks to deep reds.

## Turmeric:

Known for its health benefits, turmeric is also an excellent natural dye. Offering vibrant and warm yellow hues, this spice can be easily extracted and used to dye fabrics. I left it in for less time for one of my samples on page 153, and it gave a lighter yellow, but you can also use mordants like iron to turn the yellow more olive.

## Weld:

A flowering plant native to Europe, weld produces a brilliant yellow dye. Known for its lightfastness, making it suitable for outdoor textiles. In my sample I have added iron a modifier to make it more green/olive.

## Logwood:

The heartwood of the logwood tree produces purple and violet colours. It can create a wide spectrum of purple tones, from lilac to deep plum, adding a regal touch to any fabric or craftwork. In one of my samples, I used iron as a modifier to make the purple more of a grey.

## Cochineal:

Derived from the *Dactylopius coccus* insect found on cactus plants, cochineal is highly regarded for the vivid red and pink dyes it produces. You can also use Hibiscus flower and avocado to create various shades of pink.

## Indigo:

This plant-based dye has been used for thousands of years in many cultures, and in Japan it's associated with harmony and wisdom. It's also popular in the West, notably as the original dye for denim jeans. These days, jeans are dyed with a synthetic alternative, so make sure you buy the natural version.

# Hiding a stain with embroidery

Regular food or drink spillages can result in frequent washing which can, over time, cause fabric to become thin, weak, and prone to tearing or holes. A great way to hide stains and small holes is with a little fun embroidery, so here's my favourite go-to! The lazy-daisy stitch is a simple yet versatile embroidery stitch that can be used to add beautiful and intricate details to any fabric project, and can be combined with backstitch to create stems for your flowers.

## Things You'll Need

- **Garment to be embroidered**
- **Iron and ironing board**
- **Fusible patch (optional)**
- **Embroidery ring or hoop**
- **Air- or water-soluble marker**
- **Stranded embroidery thread (floss) in contrasting colours**
- **Sharp scissors**
- **Embroidery needle**
- **1 small coin/ruler**

## Technique for Lazy-daisy Stitch

**Prepare the item and choose the design:**

1   Ensure the surface is nice and taut on an embroidery ring. If there is a hole, you can also use this technique to embroider around the hole to make it into a flower. Prepare the hole by steam pressing any strands of fibre flat, and iron on a small patch to the back of the hole to stabilize the fabric.

2   Choose the flower design you want to embroider onto your material. Draw out your design, a simple design is recommended if you're a beginner. Don't forget to practise the stitch on a spare piece of fabric before starting on your project.

3   Trace or transfer the design onto your material. You can use a pencil or an air- or water-soluble marker specifically made for fabric. Alternatively, use a small coin to draw a circle to mark the outside of your flower.

## Did you know...

Ketchup, chocolate, and wine can notoriously stain clothes because they contain pigments and enzymes that can alter the fabric colour.

When hot liquids like coffee are spilled on clothes, the heat can cause them to penetrate the fibre and set stains. They can also cause burns and ruin the fabric texture.

Alcohol spillages will strip the colour on natural fibres when washed.

Spilling acidic foods such as citrus fruits or vinegar can damage delicate fabrics like silk or wool, causing them to break down over time.

Greasy food spills can leave oily stains that are difficult to remove and can attract dust and dirt particles that make the stain worse.

Certain fabric dyes are sensitive to some food or drink spills, which can result in permanent colour changes.

The chemicals present in some of the cleaning products used to remove stains may damage the fabric and alter the texture.

All this means that you should try to remove stains as soon as possible, before they do too much damage (see pages 26–27).

4    Choose your thread colours for the flower. You can use one colour or multiple colours to create shading or depth.

5    Begin by cutting a length of thread, around 46 cm (18 in) long, and separate it into six individual strands. Choose how many strands to use based on the thickness of your fabric and the desired thickness of your stitches, but I suggest using at least three strands to ensure the stitch stands out.

**Begin sewing:**

6    Thread your needle and tie a knot at the end. The flower petals are worked in lazy-daisy stitch. Bring the needle up through the fabric where you want to start the base of the petal, making sure the knot is against the rear of the fabric. Take the needle back down into the fabric right next to where it came out, but leave a small loop of thread on the surface when pulling the thread through.

7    Hold the loop flat on the fabric with a finger and adjust it if necessary until it's the length you want your petal to be.

8    Bring the needle back up through the fabric inside the end of the loop and make a small stitch over the loop to hold it in place. Carry on making loops in a circle until you have the desired number of petals or leaves in your design.

9. Finish the stitch by bringing the needle down through the fabric at the end of the last chain stitch and tying a knot on the back of the fabric. Trim any excess thread close to the knot.

10. Then move on to the centre of the flower design, which is worked in satin stitch. Change the colour of the thread to an alternative colour (normally yellow), thread up the needle and tie a knot. Bring the needle up through the fabric at the centre of the flower. Make a small stitch by taking the needle back down near the same spot where you started.

11. Make a second small stitch right next to the first stitch. Continue making stitches to fill in the centre circle of the flower. Once finished, bring the needle to the back of the fabric and secure it with a knot.

12. If you wish to add a stem, thread the needle with a green thread and work a line of backstitches. You can also add single lazy-daisy stitches in green for leaves.

13. Knot your thread securely to finish. Now you can add more flowers, if desired.

## Technique for Chain Stitch

This stitch is a variation of the lazy-daisy. To hand-embroider chain stitch, first thread a needle with your desired embroidery thread (floss) and knot the end. To make the first chain, bring the needle up through the fabric from the wrong side and hold the thread on the fabric. Then, insert the needle back into the same hole, creating a small loop. Bring the needle back up again, about a stitch length away from the first stitch and up through the loop. Pull gently to tighten the loop and create a chain-like stitch. Repeat this process, beginning each new chain inside the previous one, ensuring they are the same length and equally spaced. To end the stitch, make a small stitch over the end of the last loop and pass the needle through to the wrong side to secure the thread. Finally, trim the excess thread and press the fabric to flatten the chain stitches.

## Technique for Leaf Stitch

When drawing your leaf, ensure you draw a central line as this is vital to the design of the leaf stitch. To work leaf stitch, first thread a needle with your desired embroidery thread (floss) and knot the end. To make the stitch, bring the needle up through the fabric at the base in the middle of the leaf shape you want to create. Next, insert the needle back into the fabric slightly to the left of the starting point along the edge of the leaf. Then take the needle back to the central line, slightly above the initial starting point. Continue making diagonal stitches on one side of the leaf, from the central line to the edge of the leaf, making sure they are evenly spaced and gradually adjusting the length of each stitch to fit the leaf shape until you reach the tip of the leaf. Then repeat this process on the other side of the leaf, creating diagonal stitches from the centre line to the edge of the leaf until you reach back at the base. Finally, secure the thread at the back of the fabric, trim any excess, and you have successfully embroidered a leaf.

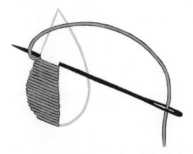

# ACKNOWLEDGEMENTS

To the makers, the visionaries, the collaborators, the ideas people, the believers, thank you for being the driving force behind the creation of this book. I want to extend a special thank you to my social media community for being my cheerleaders throughout this journey. Your belief in me has been a constant source of motivation, and I am truly humbled by your ongoing support.

To my partner Dan, your endless support and willingness to explore my dreams with me (no matter what time it is!) have been the cornerstone of this project. Your enthusiasm, creativity, and unwavering belief in my vision means the world to me and I am so grateful to have you by my side, every step of the way. And to my son, Caleb, thank you for keeping me dreaming. You're a constant reminder of the joy and wonder that fuels my creativity.

To my manager Chelsey, your faith in me from the very beginning made me believe more in myself. Thank you for making the impossible possible and for always being there to guide me through the ups and downs of this crazy journey!

To my editor Harriet, thank you for believing in what I have to say. Your expertise and insight has truly elevated this project to new heights, shaping this book alongside me, and I am forever grateful for your support.

To Kristin and Katherine, thank you for capturing my ideas so beautifully and bringing my vision to life in ways I could have never imagined. Your patience and creativity have been a true gift, and I am grateful for both of your contributions to this project.

And finally, to my family, thank you for your endless love, understanding, and patience as I poured my heart and soul into this book. Your unwavering support has been a beacon of light on this journey, and I am so grateful for you.

To each and every one of you, thank you for believing in me, supporting me, and helping me turn my dreams into reality. This book would not have been possible without you, and I am truly grateful for the incredible team that has surrounded me every step of the way.

**Managing Director** Sarah Lavelle
**Editorial Director** Harriet Butt
**Art direction and Design** Katherine Case
**Photographer** Kristin Perers
**Photographer's assistant** Aloha Shaw
**Fashion Stylist** Sofia Lazzari
**Prop Stylist** Max Robinson
**Head of Production** Stephen Lang
**Senior Production Controller** Gary Hayes

Published in 2024 by
Quadrille Publishing Limited

Quadrille
52–54 Southwark Street
London SE1 1UN
quadrille.com

Cataloguing in Publication Data: a catalogue record for this book is available from the British Library.

Text and designs © Annie Phillips 2024
Photography © Kristin Perers 2024
Design and layout © Quadrille 2024

Wavey line on pages 24, 26, 34, 63, 67, 73, 78, 98, 122, 134, 140, 145, 155, 158 © Juicy_fish on Freepik

ISBN 978 1 83783 228 6

Printed in China using vegetable- based in

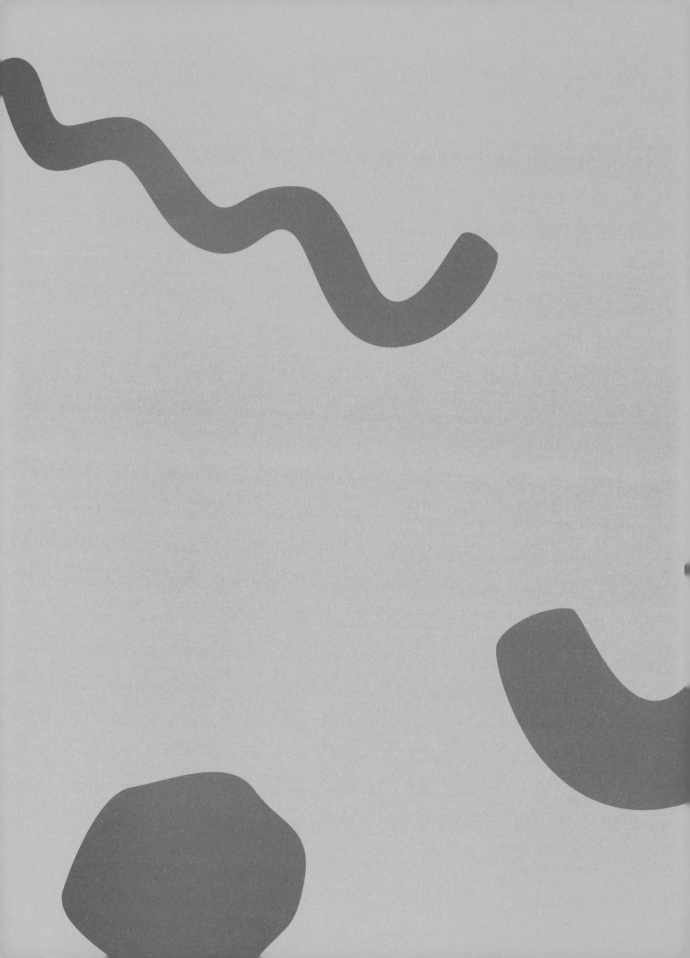